THE BONFIRE OF THE DECENCIES

The Bonfire of the Decencies

Repairing and Restoring the British Constitution

ANDREW BLICK AND PETER HENNESSY

ANDREW BLICK is professor of politics and contemporary history and head of department of political economy, King's College London. He is the author of books including *Electrified Democracy: The Internet and the United Kingdom Parliament in History* and *Beyond Magna Carta: A Constitution for the United Kingdom*. Before entering academia, he worked in the UK Parliament and at Number 10 Downing Street. His PhD on the history of special advisers in UK government was supervised by Peter Hennessy. He is senior adviser to the Constitution Society, an educational charity for the promotion of knowledge of constitutional issues.

PETER HENNESSY is Attlee professor of contemporary British history at Queen Mary University of London. He is the author of several books including a post-war trilogy (*Never Again: Britain 1945–51*; *Having It So Good: Britain in the Fifties*; *Winds of Change: Britain in the Early Sixties*). His most recent work is *A Duty of Care: Britain Before and After Covid*. He is a fellow of the British Academy and an honorary fellow of St John's College, Cambridge. He sits in the House of Lords as an independent crossbench peer.

First published in 2022 by
Haus Publishing Ltd
4 Cinnamon Row
London SW11 3TW

Copyright © Andrew Blick and Peter Hennessy, 2022

A CIP catalogue for this book is available from the British Library

The moral rights of the authors have been asserted

ISBN 978-1-913368-71-5
eISBN 978-1-913368-72-2

Typeset in Garamond by MacGuru Ltd
Printed in the UK by Clays Elcograf S.p.A.

www.hauspublishing.com
@HausPublishing

'The British constitution has always been puzzling and always will be.'

HM Queen Elizabeth II, 1992[1]

'In that faith [the Church of England], and the values it inspires, I have been brought up to cherish a sense of duty to others, and to hold in the greatest respect the precious traditions, freedoms, and responsibilities of our unique history and our system of parliamentary government. As the Queen herself did with such unswerving devotion, I too now solemnly pledge myself, throughout the remaining time God grants me, to uphold the constitutional principles at the heart of our nation.'

HM King Charles III's address to the nation and Commonwealth, 9 September 2022[2]

'People have forsaken him [Johnson] for not sticking to the rules – he hasn't bothered with them, or with respect for truth and integrity.'

Lord Mackay of Clashfern, Lord Chancellor (1987–97), 2022[3]

'I am deeply aware of this great inheritance and of the duties and heavy responsibilities of Sovereignty which have now passed to me. In taking up these responsibilities, I shall strive to follow the inspiring example I have been set in upholding constitutional government …'

HM King Charles III's Declaration, 10 September 2022[4]

'... the precious principles of constitutional government which lie at the heart of our nation.'

HM King Charles III's reply to addresses of condolence at Westminster Hall[5]

In Memory of George Jones

Friend and Teacher

Contents

Introduction

The British constitution matters. Its observance is crucial to the well-being of all our people, to every state activity and deployment of government power. The constitution is an indispensable checker and balancer of that power. It reaches still wider, for it is fundamental to sustaining the decencies of British public and political life. These in turn are crucial to the face our society presents to itself and, therefore, to the culture, character, calibre, and influence of our nation.

When working well, the peculiar – even eccentric – bundle of laws, codes, conventions, and expectations of which the constitution is comprised reflects our national appetite for decency and probity on the part of those placed in authority over us. The constitution is not an instrument to be used for narrow personal or political advantage. When working poorly, our constitutional arrangements are bringers of unease, sometimes even of a corrosive contagion. At such times it is vital for the constitution to be seen for what it is – a shared national asset. Each prime minister is its temporary guardian, *not* its sole owner. It is not their personal plaything.

The British constitution, however, for all its importance, is a thing of considerable mystery and elusiveness as the Queen indicated during her visit to a seminar at Queen Mary University of London in 1992. Michael Gove, when serving as minister for the Cabinet Office in the Johnson Cabinet, told the House of Lords Select Committee on the Constitution (on which one of us sat) in 2021 that the British state possesses a 'historically loose and baggy nature'.[1] It is indeed very hard to pin the British constitution down. It does not reside inside any set of hard covers. As the former lord chief justice, Lord Judge, once put it, ours is only a 'half written constitution'.[2]

There is another elusive factor doing its mystifying work too. For the overall functioning of the constitution has to do with states of mind. That titan of Victorian politics, W. E. Gladstone, recognised this when he wrote in 1879 that the British constitution 'presumes more boldly than any other, the good sense and the good faith of those who work it'.[3] Note those last four words of Gladstone's. For this is an early version of what later became known as 'the good chaps theory of government' – a term that should now become obsolete, though the underlying concept to which it refers remains pertinent (see box).

Recognising and defining constitutional self-regulation

Any constitutional system requires those operating within it to share a basic set of values. They must know what is and is not appropriate behaviour and be able and willing voluntarily to remain within the limits, even if to do so might not serve their narrow personal or partisan gain. In the UK, with its traditional lack of hard, judicial constitutional constraints, such self-regulation has been of particular importance. The label 'good chaps theory of government' – coined in 1985 by Clive Priestley, formerly a senior member of the prime minister's Efficiency Unit – is used to refer to this model for the operation of the UK political system.[4] We recognise that this term now seems problematic, and that an attempt to apply a label to this concept today would use different language. At the same time, while social values have changed, the importance of self-regulation – and the gravity of its failing to operate – remains. The time for the use of this particular phrase has now passed, and it should be replaced by new and more appropriate ways of describing this fundamental idea.

For multiple reasons, which we will examine in the pages to come, the decencies of government, and the constitution from which they draw (or should draw) their sap and vitality, find themselves at a low ebb in the early 2020s. Far from equipoise there is disequilibrium. There has been a serious seepage of trust, which has generated a pessimism of spirit among the British people.

We offer some thoughts as to why this is so and offer a range of suggestions about what might be done to repair and restore the British constitution. It is our belief that this is a first-order problem for the country. Time is pressing for the pursuit of what needs to be a shared national endeavour, a story of restoration, revival, and creative purpose.

Part One

The Nature of the Problem

Our central thesis is that mechanisms for the upholding of constitutional principles in the United Kingdom are deficient and require an overhaul (for a note on the existing literature to which we relate and our methodology, see Appendix 4). The experience of Boris Johnson's premiership between 2019 and 2022 has provided the focus for our exploration of this subject. He was a source of serious disruption from the outset of, and throughout, his tenure. Even the final unravelling generated uncertainties about matters such as misleading Parliament and the public;[1] confidentiality rules for former civil servants;[2] collective Cabinet responsibility;[3] the circumstances in which it is and is not appropriate to request a dissolution of Parliament from the monarch;[4] how a prime minister who is holding office only pending the selection of a replacement should conduct themselves;[5] and understandings about the holding of confidence votes in the House of Commons.[6]

But the instability that manifested itself under Johnson – however startling in itself – is part of a wider and longer continuum touching on what the writer Eleanor Updale has called 'the fragile crystal ball of the constitution'.[7] Any relief that the ending of his term as prime minister might (understandably) arouse should not distract from a realisation that urgent and substantial corrective action is required.[8] His mere departure will not reverse the damage caused during his premiership. Many changes brought about will remain in force until actively reversed, and initiatives instigated will continue to come into being unless halted. Forces, groups, and people that drove, sustained, and were harnessed by him in his anxiety-inducing conduct during this tenure can be expected to continue to exert themselves, potentially leading to further such harm. Indeed, the post-Johnson UK government will inevitably include within it numerous individuals who variously tolerated, facilitated, defended, and took a prominent role in the patterns of behaviour that made his term of office so objectionable. Ultimately, his party turned on him. But the fact that it installed him as leader at all, and that it took so long to remove him, is not encouraging. The decisive revolt of July 2022 came only after the emergence of clear evidence that he had morphed politically from asset to liability, and as a result of growing resentment among colleagues who found themselves personally compromised by some of the dubious characteristics of his administration.[9]

It is not realistic to expect politicians wholly to exclude personal and partisan considerations from their calculations. But the experience of 2019–22 could suggest that excessive weight was being attached to these concerns, in a myopic way, with a cost to the system. Johnson exposed gaps in the protective coverage of the UK constitution that allowed him to proceed in the way he did. He widened and added to these fissures in the process. They remain open to exploitation in the future by others, who may follow his unfortunate example, and even expand and multiply them further. These vulnerabilities in the system will remain until active steps are taken to end them.

Aware of the continuing dangers, we press action upon his successor at Number 10 and all politicians within the governing and opposition parties. In making recommendations, we recognise that rules and institutions are important to the functioning of a constitution, but at the same time, they depend upon a culture that is supportive of good behaviour. Rather than presenting the two aspects as separate, we treat them as closely linked. To be successful, changes in regulations and in the mechanisms for their enforcement are dependent to a significant extent upon key players being willing to abide by them. At the same time, those very measures can encourage the culture of compliance and support they require to be viable. In a best-case scenario, the Johnson experience could provide a jolt for the UK, leading it to adopt better structures, rules, and habits in pursuit of governmental good practice.

Definitions and Assessments

For the purposes of this study, we define constitutional principles as a set of values according to which governmental institutions are supposed to operate and interact with each other and the public. They are important principally as a means of ensuring that power is distributed and exercised in a legitimate fashion – that is, in a way that is consistent and commands a degree of consensus for being fair. Constitutional principles in the UK are underpinned by various rules of differing status, ranging from loose understandings through to firm laws. But, unlike most other countries, the UK famously lacks a single text formally setting out the key provisions – that is a 'written' or 'codified' constitution.[10] Yet it is possible to construct an account of what the principles are and how they are supposed to function by reference to a series of official documents. For instance, the United Kingdom Constitution Monitoring Group (UKCMG),[11] a group of senior constitutional experts and practitioners formed in 2020, has devised a set of twenty constitutional principles that it uses in its work. It draws to a large extent on texts drafted and published by, among other institutions, the UK executive (government) (see Appendix 2).

When analysing such documents, some commentators seek to distinguish and separate content they regard as being constitutional in nature from provisions they define as relating to standards and integrity.[12] However, we take the view that there is a significant overlap between the two categories. Some requirements fit within both – for instance, the stipulation that ministers must provide accurate information to Parliament, facilitating their accountability to it.[13] Moreover, constitutional principles and integrity in public life are mutually supportive. For example, the maintenance of an impartial Civil Service ensures ministers have a source of honest advice on matters including adherence to standards.[14] Equally, if ministers avoid being compromised by conflicts of interest, they are more able genuinely to fulfil their duty to act as representatives of the public, rather than covertly serving special interests.[15] As a corollary, constitutional weaknesses can translate into, and be brought about by, failures of integrity.

This connection between constitutional principles, standards, and integrity suggests a further observation that highlights the importance of our subject. Sustaining constitutional principles is an important end in its own right. But there is also a connection with substantive outcomes. Recurring themes in some of the texts discussed here involve process: that decisions should be taken in an impartial, objective, proportionate, rational, and fair way.[16] To circumvent or undermine constitutional principles of this type is to risk discarding these qualities (or perhaps to seek intentionally to do so). The result can be policy that is not only improper in itself but also self-defeating[17] – as with the scheme of attempting to deport refugees to Rwanda, adopted in 2022 despite concerns that officials reportedly raised regarding both its viability and morality,[18] and which met with legal resistance at UK level and from the European court of human rights.[19] In a sense, while a government might view constitutional norms as frustrating constraints, they can serve its longer-term interests by protecting it from its own fallibility. For instance, when the UK government behaves in a questionable way with regard to its own treaty commitments, it undermines its own 'soft power' and moral authority to exert international influence.[20] The official inquiry into the handling of the Covid pandemic, when it begins operating in full, may well reveal examples that support this point further, perhaps involving the value of giving due consideration to official advice and scientific evidence.[21] In other words, failure to adhere to constitutional standards can lead on to the gravest of consequences, including decisions that are detrimental to democracy, entail mistreatment of vulnerable groups such as refugees, and perhaps the compromising of public health.

A discussion of the constitutional aspects of the Johnson premiership and their outcomes is enhanced by an understanding of various wider dimensions. The first is historic. The system Johnson and others in his government tested to the point that its viability came into doubt was always vulnerable to abuse, and it was at times subjected to it. Troubling contemporary episodes

and patterns identified later in this book have some precedents from earlier times. We discuss, for instance, public
communication under Johnson, finding it at times to be
misleading, false, and potentially conducted in a way that
is detrimental to the standard of political discourse.[22] At
the same time, we recognise that problems of this kind
have manifested themselves – and in serious ways – previously. In the late 1930s, for example, aides to Neville
Chamberlain took part in surreptitious and discreditable
efforts to undermine the reputation of opponents to the
government's appeasement policy, including Winston
Churchill.[23] After cooperating for half a decade in government in the successful defeat of the Axis powers,
senior Labour and Conservative politicians were willing
in 1945 to draw comparisons between one another and
the Nazis. On behalf of Labour, Clement Attlee and
Herbert Morrison criticised the proposal Churchill
made for a referendum on the continuation of the coali-
tion, noting that it was a device used by their defeated
enemy;[24] meanwhile Churchill held that Labour policies would lead the party, if in government, towards the
establishment of an equivalent to the Gestapo.[25] Similarly, there are earlier instances of controversy about the
UK behaving dishonestly over major policy issues, as in
the case of the administration of Anthony Eden and the
Suez conflict of 1956.[26]

There is, therefore, some degree of precedent for problematic issues identified in relation to Johnson and his

administration, as this example of one of them shows. However, perhaps in contrast to an approach that was promoted from within the Johnson governments,[27] we regard the search for precursors not as a means of explaining away contemporary problems but of establishing how severe they have become. When placed in this perspective, while not always unique (though it sometimes was), the Johnson administration was certainly exceptional. It stands out for the way in which it generated multiple, simultaneous concerns across different areas;[28] and for the manner in which the prime minister and his colleagues resisted meaningful accountability for transgressions,[29] and sought to deny their seriousness when they became plain.[30] The period from July 2019 saw the breaking of new ground in quantitative and qualitative senses. An example that falls in the former group was the scale on which very senior civil servants abruptly left Whitehall, which seems to have been greater than in any comparable earlier period.[31] In the latter, a prominent departure from all previous experience came in April 2022, when Johnson and Rishi Sunak became respectively the first serving prime minister and chancellor of the exchequer to be made subject to criminal sanction, for breaking pandemic-related law.[32]

The forced departure of Johnson instigated in July 2022 (the immediate trigger for which is discussed below) also had exceptional features in terms of its scale and nature. It occurred when a large number of his own ministers left the government, or even called for his departure while not actually resigning themselves, coupled with public pressure from Conservative backbenchers. We should not be surprised by the spectacle of a prime minister being removed by their own party colleagues rather than the electorate.[33] But the size of the insurgency involved and needed was unprecedented. On 6 July 2022 alone, for example, sixteen ministers resigned from his government – an unequalled figure of its type for one day.[34]

Moreover, it is difficult to find any other instance of those engaged in such a manoeuvre against their own leader effectively making the question of standards of conduct publicly so central to their case for action (though they might refer to other matters also). This aspect of the Johnson removal serves to underscore the extent to which his governments were exceptional where constitutional matters – and arguably abuses – were concerned. When resigning from Cabinet as secretary of state for health and social care on 5 July 2022, Sajid Javid noted in his published letter that: 'I am instinctively a team player but the British people also rightly expect integrity from their Government.'[35] On the same day, exiting as chancellor of the exchequer, Sunak wrote that: 'the public rightly expect government to be conducted properly, competently, and seriously ... I believe these standards are worth fighting for and that is why I am resigning.'[36]

In Conservative accounts of the reasons for removing Johnson, a clear link appeared between the conduct

Johnson engaged in, and with which he was associated, and broader constitutional matters. As the Conservative politician Lord (William) Hague wrote in July 2022, 'the Conservative Party had no choice but to remove Johnson from office. His standards of governance and veracity had fallen below what reasonable people could defend'. Johnson, Hague argued, displayed 'disloyalty … to the conventions of government and institutions of government and to the massed ranks of colleagues who did their best to support him but ultimately quit in disgust or told him to go'.[37] In the previous month, the Conservative MP and former Treasury minister Jesse Norman had provided a fuller illustration of the connections between the personal conduct of the premier and wider constitutional issues involving his government, showing how bad constitutional practice could link, for instance, to the mistreatment of vulnerable people and democratic erosion. Previously a long-term ally of Johnson, on 6 June 2022 Norman wrote an open letter to the prime minister to explain that he was registering his lack of confidence in Johnson as party leader. His complaints (the substance of which we shall return to) included that:

> you have presided over a culture of casual law-breaking at 10 Downing Street in relation to Covid … your current policy priorities are deeply questionable. Breach of the Northern Irish Protocol would be economically very damaging, politically foolhardy and

almost certainly illegal ... The Rwanda policy is ugly, likely to be counterproductive and of doubtful legality. Privatisation of Channel 4 is an unnecessary and provocative attempt to address a political non-issue during a time of crisis ... No genuinely Conservative government should have supported the recent ban on noisy protest – least of all when basic human freedoms are facing the threat of extinction in Ukraine ... you are simply seeking to campaign, to keep changing the subject and to create political and cultural dividing lines mainly for your advantage.[38]

It is possible to convey the scale on which norms were undermined in the Johnson era by considering the contents of some key constitutional texts. The first is the seven principles of public life. It was issued in 1995 by the newly formed Committee on Standards in Public Life (CSPL). This body was set up by the then prime minister John Major in the autumn of 1994, in the context of growing concerns about conduct and standards among holders of high office. Referred to by Major as his 'ethical workshop', CSPL continues to operate today.[39] The text of the seven principles of public life, also commonly known as the 'Nolan principles' (named after the first chair of the Committee, Lord Nolan) is perhaps the closest equivalent the UK has to a statement of fundamental constitutional principles, though it has no hard legal force. The seven principles apply to all holders of public office.[40] The following table offers examples of challenges to, or outright violations of, the principles perpetrated by the UK government during the Johnson premiership, giving an idea of areas and themes where anxieties have arisen.

Text of the seven principles of public life (cited text in italics) with examples of questionable activities in relation to each principle occurring during the Johnson governments

Cited text	Examples of questionable behaviour
1.1 Selflessness *Holders of public office should act solely in terms of the public interest.*	• In his exercise of the office of prime minister, Johnson displayed an apparent reluctance to ensure that considerations of the wider good overrode the desire for gratification and perceived self-interest. During 2022, for instance, his desire for personal political survival seemed to take priority over all else.[41] The June 2022 accusation by Norman, cited above, that Johnson was 'simply seeking to campaign, to keep changing the subject and to create political and cultural dividing lines mainly for [his] advantage' suggested such a perception of his conduct.[42] • People around Johnson in government seemed to share his problematic approach in this area, perhaps with his encouragement, overt or otherwise. The final report by Sue Gray, the Cabinet official entrusted with inquiring into gatherings on government premises during Covid restrictions, conveyed the impression of an outlook within Number 10 according to which rules designed by the government itself to protect the public interest could be evaded – even at the risk of being exposed – in pursuit of pleasure, or in deference to pressure within their working environment to conform.[43] • Politicians willing to serve within the Johnson governments despite his manifest unsuitability for office arguably prioritised their own careers above clear public interest. The eventual mass resignation and pressure for him to resign from within the government of July 2022 were long in arriving.[44] They were probably motivated not only by principled consideration, but also by other factors, such as the sense Johnson had become an electoral and political liability.[45]

Cited text	Examples of questionable behaviour
1.2 Integrity *Holders of public office must avoid placing themselves under any obligation to people or organisations that might try inappropriately to influence them in their work. They should not act or take decisions in order to gain financial or other material benefits for themselves, their family, or their friends. They must declare and resolve any interests and relationships.*	• While clearing him of a violation of the *Ministerial Code* over the matter, the independent adviser on ministers' interests, Lord Geidt, was critical of the way in which the prime minister and officials behaved with regard to financing the refurbishment of the Number 11 Downing Street flat during 2020.[46] • In November 2021, the government attempted to intervene in such a way as to protect Owen Paterson, then a Conservative MP, from punishment for breaking parliamentary rules on lobbying.[47] In this sense the Johnson government sought actively to undermine the promotion of this principle within Parliament. • The awarding of Covid-related contracts was a source of controversy that is relevant to the integrity principle. The use of a 'VIP lane', for instance, was found unlawful in a case that reached the High Court in January 2022.[48] In July 2022, in a report into the handling of government contracts with the healthcare corporation Randox Laboratories Ltd, the House of Commons Committee of Public Accounts found that: 'During the COVID-19 pandemic, the Department of Health & Social Care (the Department) awarded contracts worth almost £777 million to Randox Laboratories Ltd (Randox) for COVID-19 testing services and goods.' The Committee complained that 'the Department's poor record-keeping means that we cannot be sure that all these contracts were awarded properly ... basic civil service practices to document contract decision making were not followed.' Furthermore, 'the Department ... failed in its duties to be transparent about meetings that its ministers had with Randox. The potential for conflicts of interest was obvious, but the Department neglected to explicitly consider conflicts of interest in its awarding of contracts to Randox.'[49]

Cited text	Examples of questionable behaviour
1.3 Objectivity *Holders of public office must act and take decisions impartially, fairly and on merit, using the best evidence and without discrimination or bias.*	• There was evidence during the Johnson governments of unusually high levels of ministerial pressure on senior public appointment processes.[50] • The Johnson administration remained committed to plans to alter legal protections for human rights (now seemingly dropped by his successor),[51] and perhaps to reduce the potential for judicial review to restrict the executive, despite commissions that it instigated failing to find such measures necessary.[52] • There is evidence that the government heavily deployed its power to make decisions about the targeting of public expenditure to secure votes in the House of Commons.[53] • The policy of attempting to deport refugees to Rwanda seemed to contradict the objectivity principle, alongside other problems with it, such as its human rights aspects.[54]
1.4 Accountability *Holders of public office are accountable to the public for their decisions and actions and must submit themselves to the scrutiny necessary to ensure this.*	• In its early phases in 2019, the Johnson administration negotiated the Northern Ireland Protocol of the European Union Withdrawal Agreement, intended as a means of reconciling the Northern Ireland Peace Process with UK departure from the European Union. Initially, the government and Conservative Party publicly presented the Withdrawal Agreement as a substantial diplomatic success.[55] Yet the administration soon came to distance itself from the Protocol, unilaterally choosing to delay implementation of parts of it, and demanding alterations to it.[56] This pattern of behaviour implied a denial of responsibility for an agreement about which Johnson had once boasted.[57] • The UK government declined fully to adopt proposals from the Committee on Standards in Public Life intended in part to strengthen independent ethical scrutiny of the executive.[58] • The critical attitude shown by members of the government towards legal processes for reviewing the activities of the executive suggested a hostility towards such scrutiny, and a desire to limit it.[59] To choose three from the numerous available examples of such conduct, in September 2019, in the wake of the *Miller II* judgment by the Supreme Court that ruled

Cited text	Examples of questionable behaviour
	an attempted prorogation of Parliament unlawful, the attorney general, Geoffrey Cox, and Johnson both made statements appearing to promote the idea of some kind of political vetting for judicial appointments.[60] In October 2020, Priti Patel, the home secretary, gave a speech in which she criticised 'do-gooders' and 'lefty lawyers'.[61] A year later, Dominic Raab, lord chancellor and secretary of state for justice, claimed in a speech that the Human Rights Act 1998 was being 'abused' by 'dangerous criminals'.[62] Providing evidence of what might have been a deliberate effort to intimidate the judiciary, Raab's predecessor, Robert Buckland, had spoken in July 2021 of how judges were showing greater 'restraint', having been 'encouraged' by the executive to do so.[63]
1.5 Openness *Holders of public office should act and take decisions in an open and transparent manner. Information should not be withheld from the public unless there are clear and lawful reasons for so doing.*	• The Johnson administration resisted publication of a report by the Intelligence and Security Committee of Parliament on Russian interference in UK politics.[64] • There was seemingly a lack of transparency surrounding the award of Covid-related contracts,[65] as the concerns raised by the Commons Committee on Public Accounts cited above suggests.[66] • Despite the passing of a Humble Address by the Commons in March 2022 that it should publish the intelligence and security agencies' advice on the possibility of a peerage (subsequently granted) for Evgeny Lebedev, the UK government refused to do so.[67]
1.6 Honesty *Holders of public office should be truthful.*	• There is evidence that the UK government negotiated the Northern Ireland Protocol in bad faith, with some first-hand accounts suggesting that figures within the administration entered into the agreement while contemplating later reneging upon it, or at least reassuring allies by telling them that it would be possible to do so.[68] • Johnson and others in his government made numerous misleading claims. For instance, from November 2021 onwards he made the same false assertion about employment figures at least nine times.[69] The Home Office made claims about the United Nations Refugee Agency (UNHCR) being involved in its Rwanda deportation policy that the agency itself denied.[70]

Cited text	Examples of questionable behaviour
	• The Johnson government provided misleading accounts about the background to the Chris Pincher episode.[71] At the end of June 2022, the Conservative MP Chris Pincher resigned as deputy chief whip following revelations about inappropriate conduct on his part. It subsequently emerged that Johnson, who had appointed him to this post in February of that year, had been briefed in 2019 about misbehaviour by Pincher when he was a minister at the Foreign Office.[72] But the existence of this prior knowledge was only made clear following an extraordinary public intervention by a former official with first-hand knowledge of the case.[73] Such was the seriousness of this episode and the way the government handled it that it was the immediate cause of the downfall of Johnson.[74]
1.7 Leadership *Holders of public office should exhibit these principles in their own behaviour and treat others with respect. They should actively promote and robustly support the principles and challenge poor behaviour wherever it occurs.*	• Sue Gray, in her report into gatherings during Covid restrictions, captured shortcomings in this area that could be applied more generally when referring to: 'failures of leadership and judgment in No 10 and the Cabinet Office'. Gray went on: 'the senior leadership and the centre, both political and official, must bear responsibility for this culture.'[75]

A second text against which it is appropriate to measure executive conduct is *The Cabinet Manual*.[76] The inaugural and to date only edition of this document appeared more than a decade ago, in 2011. However, pending the new version, which is in production,[77] it provides the fullest single official account of rules applying to the UK executive. Many of the arrangements it refers to lack direct legal force, and the manual itself purports only to describe, not create, rules. But nonetheless the provisions depicted within it are vital to the functioning of the system.[78] The doubts generated about them during the Johnson premiership are therefore worrisome.

The Cabinet Manual *(cited text in italics): selected areas of concern during the Johnson administration*

Cited text	Examples of challenges, questionable activity, or outright violations
Parliamentary democracy	
1. The UK is a Parliamentary democracy which has a constitutional sovereign as Head of State; a sovereign Parliament, which is supreme to all other government institutions, consisting of the Sovereign, the House of Commons and the House of Lords; an Executive drawn from and accountable to Parliament; and an independent judiciary.	• Early in his premiership, Johnson's administration sought – through the deployment of royal power – to compromise the ability of Parliament to hold the executive to account through a prorogation. The Supreme Court deemed this initiative 'unlawful because it had the effect of frustrating or preventing the ability of Parliament to carry out its constitutional functions without reasonable justification.'[79] • The posture of the Conservative Party and government towards the courts has helped place the judiciary in a politically exposed position.[80] Identifying tendencies that had intensified under Johnson, the All-Party Parliamentary Group on Democracy and the Constitution found in its 2022 report that: 'ministers have, from a constitutional perspective, acted improperly in attacking judges and, in particular doing so in a way that might

Cited text	Examples of challenges, questionable activity, or outright violations
	reduce public confidence in the judiciary and/or implies that ministers know better than judges on questions of fact and law.'[81]
2. *Constitutional convention is that executive power is exercised by the Sovereign's Government, which has a democratic mandate to govern. Members of the Government are normally Members of the House of Commons or the House of Lords and the Government is directly accountable to Parliament. The government of the day holds office by virtue of its ability to command the confidence of the House of Commons. Elections are held at least every five years to ensure broad and continued accountability to the people. Election candidates can stand independently but they usually represent political parties, and party numbers in the House of Commons determine the composition of the Government.*	• The repeal of the Fixed-term Parliaments Act 2011 through the Dissolution and Calling of Parliaments Act 2022 has left doubts about the understandings that apply regarding when it is and is not appropriate for a prime minister to request a dissolution from the monarch, creating more potential for abuse.[82] • The Johnson government introduced controversial legislation, the Elections Act 2022, which includes voter identification requirements that might have the effect of reducing levels of electoral participation, in particular among marginalised social groups.[83] The Elections Act also undermined the Electoral Commission in its independence from the UK government.[84] • In July 2022, the UK executive used its control over the parliamentary agenda to avoid the holding of a vote on a confidence motion framed in terms it found inconvenient.[85]
The sovereign	
6. *The Sovereign is the Head of State of the UK, providing stability, continuity and a national focus. By convention, the Sovereign does not become publicly involved in the party politics of government, although he or she is entitled to be informed and consulted, and to advise, encourage and warn ministers.*	• The attempted prorogation of 2019 exceptionally drew the prerogative powers exercised by the monarch into the centre of heightened party-political controversy, soon followed by a high-profile legal case in which the use of the powers that ministers had sought was found unlawful.[86]

Cited text	Examples of challenges, questionable activity, or outright violations
Parliament	
9. *In the exercise of its legislative powers, Parliament is sovereign. In practice, however, Parliament has chosen to be constrained in various ways – through its Acts, and by elements of European and other international law…*	• Early in his premiership, Johnson showed a lack of respect towards Parliament as a legislative body in response to its passing a law intended to constrain him in his approach to Brexit (the European Union (Withdrawal) (No.2) Act 2019). He insisted repeatedly on describing it as the 'surrender Act', despite warnings about the potentially harmful tone of such terminology.[87] Johnson also appeared to imply that he might choose not to obey this law.[88] • This paragraph suggests the existence of a principle that the deployment of the legislative supremacy of Parliament – even if this power is in theory legally unlimited – should be tempered by the objective of upholding constitutional norms. The Johnson governments, using executive influence within Parliament, pursued a legislative programme that in various ways challenged domestic constitutional principles and international law and treaty obligations.[89]
10. *Parliament also scrutinises executive action. Indeed, the government of the day is primarily responsible to Parliament for its day-to-day actions. This function is exercised through a variety of mechanisms, such as the select committee system, Parliamentary questions, oral and written statements, debates in both Houses and the Parliamentary Commissioner for Administration.*	• The Johnson executive was less than cooperative with Parliament in this oversight role, for instance through making inaccurate statements to it over issues such as crime figures.[90]

Cited text	Examples of challenges, questionable activity, or outright violations
11. By the Scotland Act 1998, the Government of Wales Acts 1998 and 2006 and the Northern Ireland Act 1998, Parliament devolved powers over areas of domestic policy such as housing, health and education to directly elected legislatures in Scotland, Wales and Northern Ireland. Parliament retains the legal power to continue to legislate on these matters, but it does not normally do so without the consent of these devolved legislatures...	• Powers taken on at UK level in the wake of departure from the EU arguably represent a relative diminution of the authority of the devolved institutions within the UK constitution.[91] • This paragraph allows for Parliament exceptionally to legislate for devolved matters without consent from devolved legislatures. However, it is not supposed to do so 'normally'. There were signs under the Johnson administration that this practice is becoming normalised, to the point that the 'not ... normally' proviso no longer holds.[92] (This rule originated as an understanding without full legal force, known as the Sewel Convention. It is now referred to in two Acts of Parliament, but it seems not to be justiciable, so is best seen as a convention, albeit one the viability of which might be in doubt.)
The prime minister and ministers	
12. Ministers' powers derive from legislation passed by Parliament, the Royal Prerogative and common law. They are subject to an overarching duty to act in accordance with the law. The courts rule on whether ministerial action is carried out lawfully...	• The Johnson governments took a confrontational stance towards the courts and their ability to review executive action and showed an interest in possible legal means of reducing their independence (see p. 22).[93]

Cited text	Examples of challenges, questionable activity, or outright violations
13. The roles of the Prime Minister and Cabinet are governed largely by convention. The Prime Minister is the Sovereign's principal adviser, chairs Cabinet and has overall responsibility for the organisation of government. Cabinet is the ultimate arbiter of all government policy; decisions made at Cabinet and Cabinet committee level are binding on all members of the Government, save where collective agreement is expressly set aside, and any minister who cannot accept them is expected to resign…	• The drive to force Johnson out of office from within his own party in July 2022 saw an unprecedented collapse in Cabinet solidarity, over the fundamental issue of the fitness of the prime minister to hold office. Some ministers declining to resign nonetheless publicly called upon him to stand down.[94]
14. Ministers have a duty to Parliament to account, and be held to account, for the policies, decisions and actions of their departments and agencies.	• The Johnson governments displayed a tendency to shift blame for shortcomings to officials, to the detriment of this principle.[95]
15. Ministers hold office as long as they have the confidence of the Prime Minister. They are supported by impartial civil servants. Civil servants are required to act with honesty, objectivity, impartiality and integrity. Ministers must uphold the political impartiality of the Civil Service, and not ask civil servants to act in any way which would conflict with the Civil Service Code and the requirements of the Constitutional Reform and Governance Act 2010.	• Johnson was criticised for the extent to which he showed confidence in some ministers regardless of evidence of their transgressions.[96] On 5 July 2022 Johnson acknowledged to journalists that making Chris Pincher deputy chief whip earlier in the year 'was a mistake' and 'in hindsight the wrong thing to do'.[97] • Revelations about lockdown gatherings provided clear examples of civil servants falling short in areas such as honesty and integrity. There are firm grounds for concluding that weaknesses on the part of political and official leadership helped bring this circumstance about.[98] • The numerous abrupt departures of senior civil servants were problematic from the point of view of principles including impartiality.[99]

Cited text	Examples of challenges, questionable activity, or outright violations
	• In July 2022, the government initially provided misleading versions of events related to the Pincher case. A former senior official therefore felt compelled to correct the record, though such behaviour amounted to a departure from confidentiality principles.[100] In a letter on 5 July to the Parliamentary Commissioner for Standards, Kathryn Stone, Lord McDonald of Salford, the former Foreign Office permanent secretary, wrote that: 'inaccurate claims by 10 Downing Street continue to be repeated in the media. On 3 July, the BBC website reported: "No official complaints against [Mr Pincher] were ever made." ... In the summer of 2019, shortly after he was appointed minister of state at the Foreign Office, a group of officials complained to me about Mr Pincher's behaviour ... An investigation upheld the complaint; Mr Pincher apologised and promised not to repeat the inappropriate behaviour ... Mr Johnson was briefed in person about the initiation and outcome of the investigation.'[101]
The judiciary	
16. The judiciary interprets and applies the law in its decisions. It is a long-established constitutional principle that the judiciary is independent of both the government of the day and Parliament so as to ensure the even-handed administration of justice. Civil servants, ministers and, in particular, the Lord	• The Johnson governments seemingly took a deliberately confrontational attitude towards the judiciary and legal processes (see pp. 22–3). The lord chancellor (and secretary of state for justice), Dominic Raab, notwithstanding the duty referred to in this paragraph (and contained in legislation setting out the oath those appointed to the post are required to swear) was a prominent proponent of this approach.[102]

Cited text	Examples of challenges, questionable activity, or outright violations
Chancellor are under a duty to uphold the continued independence of the judiciary, and must not seek to influence particular judicial decisions…	• There is evidence that, in the climate the Johnson governments helped generate, the Supreme Court became less inclined to find against the government.[103]
European Union [no longer applicable] and other international law…	
18. The UK has … ratified a wide range of … treaties that form part of the constitutional framework – for example the Charter of the United Nations, the European Convention on Human Rights, the North Atlantic Treaty and the various agreements of the World Trade Organization…	• The Johnson governments pursued initiatives and legislative measures that showed disregard for international obligations with regard to the treatment of refugees.[104] • The Johnson administration came to depict the Northern Ireland Protocol, which it negotiated, agreed, and proclaimed to voters as a success, as proving to be an unwelcome arrangement it could choose unilaterally to depart from.[105] Indeed, it may have regarded this approach as an option from the outset, and possibly privately communicated this view to those it wished to reassure on this point.[106] Acting unilaterally, the UK delayed implementing the Protocol in full.[107] The government twice introduced bills into Parliament containing provisions intended to enable it to disapply the effects of the Protocol in domestic law, generating controversy from an international law perspective.[108]
Ministerial conduct	
3.46 Ministers are under an overarching duty to comply with the law, including international law and treaty obligations…	• The prime minister and the chancellor of the exchequer were found, while in office, to have committed, on government premises, a criminal act in which others including officials were also participants. Neither resigned as a consequence.[109] • For international law and treaty obligations, see above.

Cited text	Examples of challenges, questionable activity, or outright violations
The role of ministers and officials	
7.2 … Ministers … have a duty to give fair consideration and due weight to informed and impartial advice from civil servants, as well as to other considerations and advice in reaching policy decisions.	• Whether this principle is being adhered to at a given time is to some extent a matter of judgement. But grave concerns expressed by officials appeared to be rejected in some highly sensitive areas, such as the original plan to override aspects of the Northern Ireland Protocol, reported to be the reason for the resignation of Sir Jonathan Jones, head of the Government Legal Department, in 2020;[110] and over the Rwanda refugee plan.[111]

Constitutional self-regulation

Both of the above tables help convey the scale on which departures from or challenges to norms occurred under Johnson. A realisation of the extent to which constitutional mores have lately been brought into doubt has implications for the UK system and the means by which its principles are maintained. Any political order depends to some extent on those who work within it being aware of general standards of conduct, wishing to avoid pronounced deviation from them, and seeking to promote such adherence among others around them.[112] They must be willing to prioritise the maintenance of norms over such ends as personal gratification and individual or partisan gain.[113] In the UK context, this kind of self-supervision is exceptionally important, for reasons including the absence of a 'written' or 'codified' constitution, and the need to maintain the impartiality of the monarchy.[114]

We claim neither that voluntary compliance was ever entirely effective, nor that it completely disappeared under Johnson. Nonetheless, the evidence discussed here suggests a notable lack of it within the UK government in this period. It is worth considering, therefore, what other constitutional safeguards are in place should self-regulation within the UK executive – and in particular on the part of the prime minister – fail to manifest itself. The table below sets out some of the key mechanisms, with comments on the way they operate, and their limitations. It shows that, while there are a variety of protections, they have important limitations. An absence of self-regulation, therefore, to a significant extent leaves the system exposed. When considering these various potentially countervailing forces, it is useful to refer to a theory first advanced a little over three decades ago by the late Professor George Jones, to whom this study is dedicated.[115] With a model he applied specifically to the UK premiership, Jones depicted prime ministers as subject to various constraining factors that – while allowing them a degree of flexibility – also offered resistance. Premiers might seek to stretch the restrictions, determinedly pursuing their own courses of action. But eventually the elastic would snap back into place. The further it was stretched, the more abrupt and powerful that reversion would be, potentially signalling the downfall of a prime minister.

Constitutional constraints on the UK executive and prime minister other than self-restraint

Mechanism	Comments	Limitations
Cabinet	• Internal to the executive, both full Cabinet and Cabinet committees exist to ensure that important policy decisions are discussed and agreed by ministers as a group, in a formal setting.	• Requires Cabinet members to be willing, individually and collectively, to assert themselves with respect to a prime minister or others who might be behaving improperly, perhaps to the point of threatening to resign, or actually resigning. When making decisions about whether to do so, they will probably take into account a range of considerations beyond the merits of the issue itself, such as their own careers and the standing of the government and the prime minister at a given time. • Prime ministers sometimes seek to circumvent formal Cabinet procedures, to avoid possible resistance.
The Civil Service	• In advising ministers, officials are required to bring to their attention relevant information, even if inconvenient. Ministers are required to take their views into account.	• Civil servants are not constitutionally independent from ministers and act on their instructions. They are not allowed to engage in public controversy, a prohibition which is supposed to continue after they have left their roles.

Mechanism	Comments	Limitations
	• Accounting officers can require a ministerial direction for proposed uses of public money about which they have concerns.	• Ministers may choose to rely heavily on advisers chosen from outside the permanent Civil Service, such as special advisers.
Parliament	• Acts of Parliament must be subject to full parliamentary scrutiny and approval by both Houses (with the possibility, rarely occurring in practice, of the House of Lords being bypassed, most recently over the Hunting Act 2004). • Approval from the House of Commons is needed for the Budget, and the existence of a given government depends on it possessing the confidence of the Commons. • Parliament seeks to hold the UK executive to account through such activities as debates, questions, and the work of select committees. • The Lords takes a special interest in constitutional matters (for example, it possesses a bespoke Select Committee on the Constitution). At present the Lords has no single-party majority.	• Governments normally have a majority in the Commons, reducing the chances of Parliament offering substantial resistance to them. • Government business takes priority in Parliament. • The House of Lords is limited by law, convention, and understandings in the extent to which it can obstruct the executive and the Commons. • Select committees rely mainly on soft powers. • The UK executive has various means by which it can avoid complying fully with parliamentary efforts to secure its accountability. • Through creating and deploying delegated legislation, the executive can make law subject to little or no parliamentary scrutiny.

Mechanism	Comments	Limitations
Devolved and other sub-tiers of governance in the UK	• Devolved institutions might work to influence the UK executive through structures for coordination and consultation, and hope to rely on conventions about how the UK government should engage with them. • They might seek to establish their rights via the courts. • Devolved institutions and local leaders can seek to mobilise public opinion to influence the behaviour of the UK executive.	• Arrangements for involving the devolved executives in decision-making rest on convention and practice rather than hard law. Moreover, according to established constitutional arrangements, ultimately, the UK level – via the authority of the UK Parliament – can have the final say in a dispute.
The courts	• The courts can review executive actions for their legality, and for their compliance with human rights. They can also consider whether Acts of Parliament adhere to human rights standards, and potentially declare Acts incompatible with the European Convention on Human Rights.	• The courts are likely to be reluctant to engage in intensely important and controversial political matters, and publicly to be criticised if perceived as doing so. • The courts do not have an established power to strike down an Act of Parliament, even if it violates core constitutional principles.
The monarchy	• The monarchy is, in theory, in possession of a number of important legal and functional powers, such as the ability to grant (or deny) a dissolution of Parliament, and to appoint and dismiss a prime minister.	• The monarchy is required to seek to remain above party politics and to avoid public involvement in controversy. • Only in the most extreme of circumstances would the monarch contemplate denying a dissolution to a prime minister or dismissing a premier from office.

Mechanism	Comments	Limitations
	• The monarch can discuss policy matters in private meetings with the prime minister, held weekly when Parliament is sitting. • Ministers are supposed to avoid seeking to deploy the powers of the monarchy in ways that bring them into public controversy.	
Regulatory bodies and offices	• Various entities, such as the Electoral Commission, the Information Commissioner's Office, the UK Statistics Authority, the Civil Service Commission, the National Audit Office, and the Committee on Standards in Public Life, have a role in promoting compliance with constitutional principles and rules by the UK executive. They engage in activities such as conducting inquiries, issuing reports, and in some cases making rulings.	• Such institutions may face challenges in seeking to perform their roles. They may lack, for instance, a statutory basis or other powers and resources that would enable them to function more effectively. Ministers or the prime minister might seek to avoid compliance with their findings or recommendations, or might even seek to undermine their independence. They might seek to place political allies into regulatory roles.
Documents containing rules and principles	• A variety of official texts, including the *Ministerial Code*, *Civil Service Code*, and *The Cabinet Manual*, set out constitutional principles and rules that should apply to the executive.	• These texts might (or might not) have a statutory basis, but they are not directly legally enforceable, and are at times vaguely worded. The executive drafts many of these documents itself. It can fall to ministers, and in particular the prime minister, to interpret and enforce the stipulations they contain.

Mechanism	Comments	Limitations
International law and treaty commitments	• The UK is party to a wide range of international agreements that have constitutional implications. They include various human rights conventions; the Belfast/Good Friday Agreement of 1998; and the EU Withdrawal Agreement.	• The UK legal system tends towards a dualist as opposed to a monist model. This quality means that international law is not automatically integrated into the domestic legal order. A treaty, for instance, cannot directly change domestic law unless Parliament provides for it to do so. Parliament can also legislate contrary to international law and treaty commitments, if determined to do so.
Other states and international organisations	• States such as European near-neighbours and the US may seek to apply pressure to the UK executive. • Action can be taken against the UK within the framework of any international organisation of which it is a member, such as the Council of Europe and the World Trade Organisation. • Bodies of which the UK is not a member – notably the European Union – can seek to persuade and even take measures against the UK if the executive takes courses of action to which they object.	• States and international organisations are generally unlikely to involve themselves in a detailed way in the internal business of a country. Because of the dualist tendency in the UK constitution discussed above, any treaty commitments on which UK participation in organisations or arrangements rests do not have direct force in UK law, unless specifically incorporated into it, and bodies such as the UK government and UK Parliament are responsible for internal decisions. Action to force states to comply with agreements, even if successful, is likely to take place over an extended timeframe. • External interventions in the UK – such as those in which Russia and those acting on its behalf might have engaged (see p. 20) – might have the effect of undermining rather than upholding constitutional standards.

Mechanism	Comments	Limitations
Parties	• A governing parliamentary party can apply informal influence on its leadership, and may have the ability to remove a leader who is transgressing basic norms. • The views of party members beyond Parliament, perhaps on constitutional issues, can have an influence. • Opposition parties can seek to place constitutional issues on the political agenda if they choose.	• Many in a party will be inclined to defer to a leader, rather than engage in potentially damaging disputes. • Where sections of a party do assert themselves in relation to a constitutional issue, it might be to encourage or force the leadership to adopt rather than avoid problematic policies. • A party will be reluctant to deploy the ultimate sanction of removing an offending leader. Its willingness to do so is likely to vary in accordance with other factors, such as whether that leader is judged to have become an electoral liability.
The public	• Members of the public can influence the behaviour of the UK executive with respect to the constitution through voting in elections and referendums, and through the opinions they hold on constitutional issues, as discerned through opinion research. They can also be politically active, for instance through party membership or participation in campaigns. There is, too, a strong instinct for fairness in the UK.	• Members of the public will not necessarily have extensive knowledge of or interest in constitutional issues. They should not necessarily be expected to use their votes purely on a basis of such matters. An election is devalued if it becomes dominated by questions of how to prevent abuse of the system, rather than decisions about matters such as values and policy preferences. • The public has to wait until general elections take place (at intervals of up to approximately five years) before it can remove a government.

Mechanism	Comments	Limitations
		• The UK electoral system delivers disproportionate results. Consequently, even if a majority of voters specifically reject a party that gives rise to constitutional concerns, it might win a Commons majority regardless. • Some members of the public might find a rule-breaking politician or a 'populist' type programme attractive. Opinion polling presents a mixed picture regarding how far the public value integrity or the extent to which they feel willing to support a leader who achieves desired outcomes, even if violating norms in the process.[116]
The media	• The media can play a part in scrutinising, investigating, and discussing the activities of the UK executive, including from a constitutional perspective. They can promote general awareness of constitutional issues.	• The media might not have the resources or access to information required to fully scrutinise constitutional issues. They might not deem these issues of sufficient interest to their audiences. Constitutional questions of their very nature can be cloudy, even opaque, and clothed in deeply unexciting language. Media outlets might also have political agendas of their own that lead them to avoid criticism of problematic activity by the government. They may support such initiatives, or even campaign for them to be pursued. Coverage can be misleading or inaccurate, intentionally or otherwise.

Mechanism	Comments	Limitations
		Governments often seek to influence the media to produce content more favourable towards them, and may attempt to pressurise or intimidate public service broadcasters.
Civil society	• Various pressure groups, campaigns, interest groups, and institutions can exert pressure upon a government, potentially in constitutional areas.	• Such entities do not have direct power over the government, and the extent to which a government is likely to take their positions into account will vary considerably. Forces from within civil society may pursue malign as well as desirable constitutional outcomes.
Prominent public figures	• Religious leaders, senior statespersons, former officials, business leaders, or cultural figures might make interventions opposing problematic behaviour and initiatives.	• Such figures have only 'soft' power, and may be reluctant to engage because of the hostility doing so can prompt. • Public figures can also intervene to encourage or defend problematic courses of action.
Economic and financial forces	• A government seriously violating constitutional principles, for instance with regard to treaty commitments, might find itself subject to market pressures in response, or might become involved in what is popularly known as a 'trade war'.	• Such pressures are indirect, and only likely to become powerful in extreme circumstances.

Of the various constraints upon the prime minister and the executive set out above, some resisted the Johnson governments' defiance of constitutional expectations. These included the courts, elements of the UK

Parliament, and public figures. But only a small number of the limiting forces described above have the power to bring about the removal of a prime minister from office (such as the ruling parliamentary party, and Cabinet members, if enough of them act together). Eventually – but after much procrastination – some of these forces coalesced to this end in July 2022. Members of the public (especially those voting or declining to do so in by-elections); the Conservative Party in Parliament; and ministers – by resigning or exerting pressure from within government – combined to cause Johnson's position to become untenable. It is fair to say that these different groups were reacting in part to the negative constitutional consequences of the Johnson premiership, although there were other factors at work. The time it took to reach this point allowed much that was objectionable to transpire. In the process, some of the elastic limits upon the premiership were arguably weakened, possibly in a lasting way. For instance, the courts were made subject to political pressure. Furthermore, the potential for members of the public to assert themselves against the government was possibly reduced through interference with the right to protest[117] and measures that might have a negative effect on democratic electoral processes.[118] During the Johnson premiership, moreover, what was once a powerful restraint upon the discretion of the UK prime minister and executive – that provided by membership of the European Union and its

law – was consciously removed through the implementation of Brexit.[119]

We can conclude from this discussion that, while the
UK constitution is not wholly dependent upon self-
regulation by senior figures, this form of constraint is
an embedded part of the UK system, and the less per-
vasive it becomes the more vulnerabilities will appear.
We argue here that just such a malfunction was manifest
during the Johnson premiership, on the part of the prime
minister himself and others, some of whom will outlast
him in positions of senior responsibility. The range of
non-compliance with constitutional standards we identify in this book supports this view. To offer one example
here, the final Sue Gray report into gatherings on official
premises during a time of Covid restrictions, published
in May 2022, provided evidence of a lack of respect for
rules among those from whom it is most essential. Gray
described, for instance, how the principal private secretary to the prime minister sent a WhatsApp message
suggesting that 'we seem to have got away with' an event
on 20 May 2020 in the Downing Street garden.[120] It
might seem a relatively trivial remark in itself. But we
must attach wider significance to it, prompting as it
should the realisation that a person in such a position
could regard – and, in writing, encourage and reinforce
others in perceiving – activities that might be illegal as
something to be 'got away with'.

It must be noted, nonetheless, that there were signs

the system of voluntary adherence to basic standards and precepts was potentially under strain long before Johnson became prime minister in 2019. For instance, they are detectable in the growing tendency for the UK government (and other branches of the constitution) to produce various statements of principles applying to its operation.[121] During the course of the twentieth century, documents such as *Questions of Procedure for Ministers*,[122] the *Precedent Books*,[123] and *Estacode*[124] (a compilation of guidance for civil servants) sought to fix rules in writing (or at least draw them together into a unified whole), representing a shift away from a more tacit and diffuse system. Initially such texts tended to be for internal use only, and their very existence as well as contents could be secret. But by the 1990s there had been a clear shift towards publication.[125] For instance, the government made *Questions of Procedure for Ministers* public in 1992 (superseded by the *Ministerial Code* in 1997);[126] and published the *Civil Service Code* in 1996.[127] This decade also saw, as noted above, the formation of CSPL (in 1994), followed (in 1995) by its public issuing of the *Seven Principles of Public Life*.[128]

We can view this process of codification as an attempt to shore up the system of voluntary compliance. The texts involved were not generally intended to create legal obligations; they have tended to lack a statutory basis and have often not benefited from fully independent enforcement mechanisms.[129] They are a series of ad hoc accretions rather than an ironclad plan. The appearance of these various documents might be seen as beneficial to the promotion of constitutional good practice and public confidence in the system. They might be regarded as enhancing awareness of key rules and principles among both office holders and outside observers. Through this route, the likelihood of their being adhered to might increase. So might the potential for the external identification of transgressions and holding those perpetrating them to account, creating a deterrent for such activity. The rules might become more fully adhered to.[130]

But such documents are perhaps more the symptom of a problem than a means of improving it. Moreover, the extents to which they can solve problems and avoid creating further difficulties are debatable.[131] The perceived need to encapsulate rules in writing, and then to make them publicly available, was suggestive of a decline in implicit, trust-based forms of regulation.[132] The establishment of CSPL, for example, was prompted by concerns and controversies about improper conduct by politicians,[133] known at the time as 'sleaze'.[134] Another manifestation of this trend came in 1997 when both the House of Commons and House of Lords passed a motion asserting the principle that the government should be open in its dealings with Parliament, providing accurate information and supporting its efforts to achieve executive accountability.[135] (Two-and-a-half decades later, this text, reproduced as a crucial component of the *Ministerial*

Code, lay at the centre of criticism of the Johnson governments.[136]) That Parliament needed to iterate such a principle was suggestive of declining trust on its part in the executive.[137] Furthermore, the body of different documents that has become available is too great for any one individual to be fully aware of.[138] For even the most energetic hunter-gatherer of constitutional texts, tedium can set in early. The documents can create or add to ambiguity and confusion as well as clarity and certainty.[139] Moreover, if individuals who are supposed to be subject to them are determined to ignore or circumvent the rules contained in these documents, the lack of independent enforcement appears a problem.[140] If they are, in turn, perceived by the public as being ineffective, then – far from being enhanced – public trust in the system might be undermined.[141]

Recent events suggest that, despite such codification initiatives, the extent of reliance on self-regulation is a problem and requires reconsideration. The Johnson government tested the existing framework in a number of ways and – as is discussed below – pursued a policy of loosening those constraints that do exist.[142] As we have noted, there was a pre-existing tendency towards weakening of the model for constitutional regulation. Fully explaining this pattern is a considerable task. But at this point we can observe that, although our focus here is on ministers (and to some extent officials) and their conduct, a complete examination of this tendency would take in other factors. It would note, for instance, that views of declining standards might partly be a matter of perception. There may have been a long-term shift towards closer scrutiny of government, which is often likely to become critical in nature, and more official information is in the public domain.[143] From this perspective, problems were being exposed in greater numbers rather than actually multiplying. Furthermore, social expectations may have changed. Behaviour that was once more likely to be tolerated – such as bullying – is now less so.[144]

It could also be a matter of relative more than absolute change. Some would argue that while various bodies outside government have become more regulated, the executive has failed to keep pace. For example, the Nigel Boardman review into the use of supply chain finance in government, which reported in 2021, found that:

> The Civil Service has tended, in governance and compliance developments, to lag behind other institutions that are subject to greater external pressures, and has remained self-regulatory where other organisations have moved towards a more structured regulatory framework. The 'patchwork' approach to the ethics system ... needs to be streamlined and stronger, with more consistent enforcement applied.[145]

Aside from such broader questions, by 2016, the constitution and the system of self-regulation that is such an important component of it were under pressure and scrutiny. Reflecting on the experience of the period since this point, Dominic Grieve, the former Conservative Attorney General, told the House of Lords Select Committee on the Constitution in July 2022 that:

> one has to accept that we are in a tumultuous period of our politics, partly because of decisions that were taken over the last five years that, because they have a revolutionary component to the country's future, have caused ripples of disturbance right through the system. There is no reason to suppose that that will not settle down. I think it may. It may not. The United Kingdom may break up. You can think of all sorts of things that may flow from it. It has been a disturbed period, and I have experienced it at first hand in politics. That is not to say that there will not be a settlement back when people start behaving and respecting the conventions and realising their advantages.[146]

At the centre of the disruption to which Grieve referred was the taking and implementation of the decision for the UK to depart from the EU, or Brexit. The experience of Brexit added to existing constitutional uncertainties, creating turbulence around prevailing understandings. It did so by turning the system against itself. One source of disruption arose from an exercise in *direct* democracy – the 23 June 2016 EU referendum – producing a 'leave' result that majorities in both Houses of the central UK institution of *representative* democracy, Parliament, had opposed.[147] Measured by percentage, the outcome of the vote was relatively close, highlighting and augmenting sharp social and territorial divisions, which would – among other consequences – create challenges for the cohesion of the Union.[148] Resolving the many practical and political challenges connected to bringing about departure from the EU was inevitably a general strain.[149] The parliamentary arithmetic produced by the 2017 general election complicated matters further. It entailed the executive coming increasingly into conflict with the legislature, and in particular the House of Commons, the confidence of which the government rested upon.[150]

The executive also lost two landmark constitutional cases in the Supreme Court, in 2017 and 2019.[151] The second of these judgments – which related to actions perpetrated by Johnson after he became prime minister – concerned the attempted prorogation of Parliament of August 2019, subsequently determined unlawful.[152] This episode brought the monarchy closer to involvement in party political controversy than was wholly comfortable.[153] As well as coming into conflict with the law, the governing Conservative Party and Cabinet experienced internal divisions. Maintaining the principle of collective responsibility became a challenge.[154] A Cabinet member who proved particularly prone to undermining the public united front that ministers are supposed to present was Boris Johnson, foreign secretary from 2016 to 2018.[155] Describing the conduct of Johnson while foreign secretary, Gavin Barwell, a former Conservative MP who, after losing his seat at the 2017 general election, became chief of staff to Prime Minister Theresa May, referred to 'his repeated habit of briefing the press in ways that were contrary to government policy ... Government couldn't function if everyone behaved like that, but he didn't appear to believe that the rules should apply to him.'[156]

The political and constitutional turbulence Johnson helped generate in connection to Brexit would eventually bring him the premiership. The same ferment, having propelled Johnson to Number 10, provided a defining background against which he would practise his persistent and extensive defiance and erosion of norms.[157] In this sense the person, the methods used, and the Brexit policy congealed into a single political agenda. Among those operating within and commenting on politics, support for Johnson as prime minister and for Brexit were likely to come together, and could lead on to a defence of his constitutional approach.[158] Confirming this conglomeration of associations, those who adhered to it were prone to depicting concerns about the conduct of Johnson and his government as part of an anti-Brexit agenda.[159] In this sense, the issues we assess here were more than incidental if regrettable lapses. Linked to the socio-political polarisation that Brexit revealed and helped magnify, they were

part of a coherent programme pursued and promoted by
leaders and supporters alike.[160]

Populism and backsliding: The international perspective

There is also a wider international context. Three decades
ago, assessments of the global prospects for democracy
were often optimistic in tone.[161] The widespread collapse
of Communism was perceived as part of a wider pattern of
movement away from authoritarian government that
had begun in Greece, Portugal, and Spain in the early to
mid-1970s, before spreading around the world. It became
known as the third historic wave of democratisation, taking
in Europe, Asia, the Americas, and Africa (the first wave,
inaugurated by the American and French revolutions, is
regarded as running from the late eighteenth to early twentieth centuries, while the shorter second wave, lasting for a
decade or so, began at the end of the Second World War).[162]
But during the course of the twenty-first century, momen-
tum was seemingly lost. Now the mood is one of sustained
pessimism.[163] Autocratic states such as China and Russia
persist and assert their influence in various ways. Countries
that had shifted towards democracy – such as Hungary –
have now begun to regress. More established democracies
– including India, the United States, and France – also
face challenges from political leaders and movements that
appear to contest previously prevailing principles.[164]

When we assess the Johnson governments and their constitutional and political impact, it is useful to relate it to this tendency towards democratic backsliding, as it is sometimes known.[165] In particular, we should consider the contemporary UK as possibly fitting within the third group indicated above: states previously believed to be stable, which now seem to be rickety. There are many dimensions to such a discussion, which extends beyond those who held ministerial office at UK level from 2019.[166] However, the focus on Johnson and his governments is of particular value. In this respect we follow Anne Applebaum in her assessment of the way in which, across different countries, more extreme positions in areas such as immigration policy and the status of the judiciary have become part of the mainstream political right. Applebaum notes that, while the right is not the only portion of the political spectrum to have experienced change, it calls for close attention since its politicians so often manage to secure high political office. This principle applies to the UK and the Johnson governments, as Applebaum recognises.[167]

We acknowledge that there are many aspects of our political system and culture, beyond merely Johnson and his governments, that should be analysed from democratic (and other) points of view. For instance, intimidation of public office holders is a troubling tendency,[168] and a related issue – that of the impact of the internet and social media upon politics – has in recent years generated much controversy in the UK and internationally.[169] Before Johnson came to office, some detected a worrying change in the nature of UK politics, connected but not confined to Brexit. Gavin Barwell, writing from the standpoint of chief of staff to Theresa May at Number 10 from 2017–19, recalled how:

> Each time the prime minister made a statement to the House of Commons on Brexit, I would listen from the box for civil servants in the corner of the chamber and notice that the mood felt a bit more polarised. But this wasn't limited to Brexit – there was a growing populism on both the left and the right, a new generation of media commentators whose modus operandi was to foster division. And people in elected office were suffering an increasing amount of abuse on social media. To paraphrase Vice-Admiral Beatty's famous remark at the Battle of Jutland, it felt like there was something wrong with our politics.[170]

Yet while this subject is a broad one, during the period in which they formed the government of the UK, Johnson and the Conservative Party provided much material deserving of the close attention given to it here. To consider the UK as possibly comprising part of a wider pattern of democratic deterioration is – and should be – an uncomfortable task. But regrettably we identify cause for concluding that it does. We identify a number of tendencies that conform to more general models of 'backsliding' and 'populism'.[171] They include the following unlucky thirteen:

- A leader of cult-like aura, whose flaws manifest themselves in constitutionally problematic ways, which supporters of that person inside and outside government either deny, seek to explain away, claim to be outweighed by other merits, or even present as somehow positive qualities;[172]
- A practice of presenting various groups, ranging from refugees to the Civil Service, as threats or problems, and of addressing these supposed difficulties in ways that in turn create concerns about a departure from established constitutional norms.[173] For instance, refugee policy under Johnson was criticised as both stigmatising some of those who were subject to its provisions and for its implications from the point of view of adherence to international obligations;[174]
- Denigration of lawyers and legal processes, and reported interest in measures that could have the effect of weakening mechanisms for the legal oversight of the actions of the executive;[175]
- Demeaning treatment of Parliament and making attempts to compromise its ability to perform its proper functions, including holding the executive to account;[176]

- Specific initiatives with a harmful effect on human rights such as the right to protest; and wider plans to dilute measures for the overall protection of human rights;[177]
- A lax attitude among office holders towards domestic law, with both unlawful and illegal conduct by the occupants of the highest ministerial offices;[178]
- Showing less than proper regard for treaty commitments and international law, and possibly violating them outright;[179]
- Challenges to the status and impartiality of public institutions and office holders,[180] including political pressure upon appointments processes;[181]
- A weakening of mechanisms intended to protect electoral processes, and the implementation of measures that could have the effect of reducing the level of public participation in elections, particularly among excluded groups;[182]
- Problems with processes for the disbursal of public money;[183]
- The dissemination of misleading information, a compromising of the quality of public discourse, and the undermining of public service broadcasters.[184] Labelling measures in ways that deceive as to their true purpose,[185] and accusing others of problematic conduct that the administration was in fact itself carrying out or contemplating;[186]

- Violation of norms relating to good conduct in public office, and disdain for mechanisms intended to ensure compliance with them;[187] and
- The deployment of language and concepts associated with extremist conspiracy theories, for instance, the reference Johnson made in July 2022 to the 'deep state'.[188]

When attempting to justify behaviours of the type described above, those speaking on behalf of the UK government tended to refer to a need in some sense to fulfil the will of the people in the face of elite obstructions, thereby conforming further to a populist template. For instance, in a speech in which Lord Frost (while still a serving minister) rejected in its existing form and way of operating a crucial component of the EU Withdrawal Agreement, the Northern Ireland Protocol, for which he had been chief UK negotiator, he explained:

> I don't see anything wrong with Brexit being described as a populist policy. If populism means doing what people want – challenging a technocratic consensus – then I am all for it. To suggest that there is something wrong in people deciding things for themselves is somewhat disreputable, even disrespectful to the British people and our democracy.[189]

We are conscious that, at various points in the past,

observers have claimed democracy to be under threat both in general and in the UK specifically.[190] We also recognise that such concerns should not be raised lightly. However, as suggested above, the combined quantity and quality of problems manifesting themselves makes it appropriate at this point to consider the possibility of a systemic failure. Concerns held in earlier periods may or may not have been well founded. It could be that those who have previously identified problems were correct to do so, and by drawing attention to them helped correct them or prevent them from becoming worse in their eras. If we can contribute a little to a similar function in present times then we will have achieved our purpose. We wish to avoid alarmist claims about an imminent lurch in a populist or even authoritarian direction, which serve to distract from the more balanced assessment of real problems. Regardless of how far the process of deterioration we identify will progress, and irrespective of where it might ultimately lead, we have already reached a set of circumstances that are, in our view, sufficiently anxiety-inducing to require the attention we give them here. Our subject is of particular interest given that the UK is often held as an example of democratic stability and continuity, having avoided both external conquest and severe domestic disruption to democratic processes.[191] Problems for the UK are therefore significant to our wider understanding of democracy.

That the government at the centre of this discussion is Conservative is of particular significance. The ability of the Conservative Party to adapt to and reconcile itself with mass participation politics from the nineteenth century onwards features in some analyses as crucial to the stable development of democracy in the UK. Parties of the right tended, by tradition, to be defenders of privilege and traditional social structures, which could lead them to be hostile to the adoption of a more democratic system. The Conservatives, however, proved able to adjust to this change. Some accounts suggest that the lack of a party of the right with this capacity helps explain why other countries saw less steady progress than the UK.[192] From this standpoint, for the Conservative Party to take on a more hostile posture towards features of representative democracy is an occurrence of exceptional – and worrisome – importance. There is some precedent for the Conservatives showing a willingness to destabilise the system, as when they were excluded from power for a decade from 1905.[193] A difference now is that they hold office, although in some respects implementing ideas developed during the long period of opposition of 1997–2010.[194] A diverse range of observers have felt motivated to express concern about the current direction of the Conservatives in power, linking it to wider international tendencies. Some are from outside the party. For instance, the outgoing Labour peer and renowned filmmaker, Lord (David) Puttnam, spoke in October 2021 of 'the multiple dangers faced by democracy'. Puttnam held that 'not only does the world in general find itself in a bad place', but that the UK was on a specific difficult path of its own. Discussing what he saw as objectionable initiatives emerging from the UK government, Puttnam observed that:

> with every passing month there are more – each of them setting out to chip away at and undermine much of what defines an active liberal democracy: those institutions that might act as checks and balances on a populist government that's trampling on long held rights and conventions, with the sole purpose of tightening its own grip on power.[195]

Similar criticisms were more startling because of the source from which they emanated. In a February 2022 speech, the 1990–7 Conservative prime minister, (Sir) John Major, whose efforts to promote standards in the 1990s we have already encountered, cautioned: 'In many countries, there is a widespread discontent of the governed, and democracy is in retreat. Nor is it in a state of grace in the UK.' Speaking at a time of ongoing revelations about what would transpire to be illegal gatherings on official premises including Number 10 Downing Street during the pandemic, Major noted that:

> Our democracy has always been among the strongest and most settled in the world … It relies also upon respect for the laws made in parliament; upon an independent judiciary; upon acceptance of the

holder of the office chooses to operate.[198] Moreover, when considering issues of the kind addressed in this work, the premier is of exceptional importance. They take a lead on matters of a constitutional nature, and on defining and enforcing ethics and standards of conduct (as well as various other sensitive activities such as overseeing the work of the intelligence and security agencies; handling foreign relations; and conducting communications with the monarch).[199] Indeed such is their centrality to these responsibilities that it is reasonable to hold that the robustness of the political system rests on the assumption of confidence in the personal integrity and probity of the prime minister. The existence of credible concerns in this regard will inevitably compromise the effectiveness – perceived and actual – of mechanisms for the upholding of constitutional values. A good illustration of the centrality of the premier in these areas is found in paragraph 1.6 of the *Ministerial Code*, with the statement that: 'Ministers only remain in office for so long as they retain the confidence of the Prime Minister. He is the ultimate judge of the standards of behaviour expected of a Minister and the appropriate consequences of a breach of those standards.'[200]

The significance of the premier as stipulated in the code and the discretion it vests in this particular role was demonstrated in 2020, when the home secretary, Priti Patel, became the subject of an investigation by Sir Alex Allan, independent adviser on ministers' interests, into her behaviour towards civil servants and whether she had violated the code. Allan was appointed to this post in 2011, on the discretion of the prime minister, in a closed process, as was – and is – the standard method of recruitment to the office of adviser. In a 2012 report, the Public Administration Select Committee of the House of Commons (PASC), of which Patel was then a member, complained about this practice and its outcome. PASC held that:

> For the role to be independent, the appointment process was flawed, and so, unfortunately, was the choice of individual to fill that post. Any successful candidate for a post requiring independence from Government must be able to demonstrate that independence. Sir Alex Allan, as a recently retired senior civil servant, was therefore never likely to be an appropriate choice, and his evidence to us did nothing to convince us otherwise.[201]

In the evidence session referred to, among other PASC members, Patel had raised questions about 'the lack of competition for your appointment' and therefore 'what special qualities you think you have to qualify for this role'. She also asked, taking into account that the adviser could only investigate possible breaches of the *Ministerial Code* at the request of the prime minister and not on their own initiative, whether 'you feel in your current role that you are actually able to challenge those around you, including the Prime Minister, if you hear or see of anything untoward that needs to be drawn to his attention?'[202] Patel had identified genuine faults in the system. But when she herself came under investigation in 2020, they were not the problem. Under public pressure (in February, the permanent secretary at the Home Office, Sir Philip Rutnam, had resigned in acrimony), Allan was asked to carry out an inquiry in March of that year.[203] Both his findings and his response to the way in which Johnson received them demonstrated that Allan was able to act with a degree of independence. Where the system fell short on this occasion was at the prime-ministerial level.

In the report he published in November 2020, Allan, though couching his conclusion in qualifications, nonetheless held that:

> the Home Secretary has not consistently met the high standards required by the Ministerial Code of treating her civil servants with consideration and respect. Her approach on occasions has amounted to behaviour that can be described as bullying in terms of the impact felt by individuals. To that extent her behaviour has been in breach of the Ministerial Code, even if unintentionally.[204]

A five-paragraph response from the government contained the view that:

as the arbiter of the code, having considered Sir Alex's advice and weighing up all the factors, the Prime Minister's judgement is that the Ministerial Code was not breached.

The Prime Minister has full confidence in the Home Secretary and considers this matter now closed.[205]

Following Johnson's decision in November 2020, Allan responded with a brief resignation statement.[206] As Johnson had noted, as premier he was the arbiter of the code, and – aside from how well other parts of the system were or were not performing – his approach was critical to its effectiveness. Prime ministers can, if they choose and feel able to, take a firm line in enforcing standards of conduct, as, for instance, Theresa May seems to have done in circumstances leading to the resignation of Patel from a previous Cabinet role of secretary of state for international development, in November 2017.[207] In November 2020, Johnson chose to support his minister over the views of his adviser, and insist there had been no breach.

The inclinations of the person who occupies the post of prime minister, then, matter; and it is possible to identify a series of features of his approach that are relevant to the problems we identify with the Johnson governments. No doubt, to varying extents, he shares them with some other politicians, past and present. But the brazenness with which he advertised and acted upon his proclivities consistently during the course of his career, up to and including his tenure at Number 10 (and – we can reasonably anticipate – thereafter), was exceptional.[208] Moreover, controversy about his fitness for office arguably became *the* defining feature of public debate about his premiership,[209] and provided the final trigger for his removal (though we should not attribute his ousting to any one cause).[210] It might be argued that perceptions of Johnson mislead since they amount to an image he has deliberately projected, with media assistance, rather than the reality.[211] There can be no doubt that Johnson has devoted much effort to the construction of a persona. But it is also reasonable to assume that it has some relationship to his actual personality. Furthermore, irrespective of the extent to which the visible Johnson is an artifice, it is a role that he plays enthusiastically, in the process contributing to many of the problems we consider in this work.[212]

One notable Johnson trait is a studied lack of seriousness in his approach to politics, and an apparent tendency to see it principally as a means for his personal fulfilment.[213] These qualities might help explain his casual attitude to established rules and mechanisms for their maintenance, which Johnson might regard as tiresome constraints to which he need not submit himself. In 2004, a collection of articles by Johnson were published featuring a specially commissioned profile of him by a fellow journalist and future Conservative Cabinet member, Michael Gove. Gove recalled the moment at which their complex relationship began, describing 'the first time I met Boris Johnson. It was in the bar of the Oxford Union. I was a bewildered fresher and Boris was doing then what he has done superbly ever since – making people laugh and then asking for their votes.' In the interview that followed, Johnson explained to Gove that his decision to instigate a political career:

> was a manifestation of my intensifying mid-life crisis. I'd begun to feel that journalism, though I love it and I love journalists, just wasn't enough ... Journalism is very difficult to keep up at a high standard over a long period ... And in any case I felt a need to do something different.

Johnson did suggest that he had some objectives beyond simply a desire for variety and reluctance to meet the demands of a profession. As he put it to Gove, he 'felt a need to stop kicking over sandcastles and build a few of my own'. Johnson recognised that, in contrast to journalism, 'in politics ... you have to make the right decision rather than find an amusing or provocative angle'. Commenting on fellow politicians, he said he was 'constantly impressed by their dedication to the task'. Yet it seemed he did not judge himself to share this quality. He described how 'sometimes in the chamber I'll sit there amazed at the diligence colleagues show in getting to grips with an important piece of legislation and I feel rather ashamed when I do my glib Oxbridge thing – delivering a speech which is really just skating at high speed over the thinnest of ice'.[214]

Johnson, then, saw the practice of his craft in contrast to other politicians with their focus on detail. In this account he depicted the difference as a failing on his part. But in some of his writing we encounter a different theme: that of a commendably colourful politician who is unlike others, who in some sense departs from norms and codes, and is for this very reason superior to others, and whose behaviour, however flawed, should therefore be tolerated and even celebrated. In a profile of Silvio Berlusconi that appeared in *The Spectator* on 6 September 2003, Johnson reached the following conclusion:

> after decades in which Italian politics was in thrall to a procession of gloomy, portentous, jargon-laden partitocrats, there appeared this inflorescence of American gung-hoery. Yes, he may have been involved in questionable business practices; he may even yet be found out and pay the price. For the time being, though, it seems reasonable to let him get on with his programme. He may fail. But then ... he can be rejected by the Italian people.[215]

Here Johnson, it would later transpire, was rehearsing aspects of the defence he and allies offered for himself two decades later. During his premiership they conveyed the impression of an exceptional individual who should be allowed to continue their important work notwithstanding objections to their conduct,[216] and of someone in possession of a mandate bestowed specifically upon him by the public, with which elites should not be permitted to interfere.[217] Johnson held that critics of Berlusconi 'may not like it but he was democratically elected and can be removed by the very people' who his opponents, Johnson claimed, insulted. Were he, Johnson wrote, 'obliged to compare Silvio Berlusconi with … bossy, high-taxing European politicians … as the narrator [Nick Carraway] says of Jay Gatsby, a man Berlusconi to some extent resembles, he is "better than the whole damn lot of them".'[218]

A similar character, in a different guise, appears in Johnson's 2014 book on Churchill, a political hero of his whom he has seemingly aspired to emulate[219] or at least invite comparison with.[220] Seeking to explain the contribution Churchill made during the Second World War, Johnson writes:

> He knew how to project his personality, and the war called for someone who could create an image of himself – decisive, combative, but also cheery and encouraging – in the minds of the people. Churchill alone was able to do that, because to a great extent he really was that character.

Johnson, then, depicted Churchill as playing a manufactured role, but one that was nonetheless close to his own personality, and that he deployed as a political tool:

There is a sense in which eccentricity and humour helped to express what Britain was fighting for – what it was all about. With his ludicrous hats and rompers and cigars and excess alcohol, he contrived physically to represent the central idea of his own political philosophy: the inalienable right of British people to live their lives in freedom, to do their own thing.

As he did with Berlusconi, Johnson praised Churchill by contrasting him with what he depicted as duller counterparts. Johnson wrote that: 'you only had to look at Churchill, and see the vital difference between his way of life and the ghastly seriousness and uniformity and pomposity of the Nazis. Never forget: Hitler was a teetotaller, a deformity that accounts for much misery.' To depict the matters at stake in the Second World War by reference to differing lifestyle options was a questionable device that risked trivialising the issues involved. This account was, furthermore, suggestive in the author of a belief in the self-defined exceptional political leader. Johnson recognised that the approach Churchill took could create difficulties, but he maintained that when the stakes were at their highest it was not merely acceptable but vital. He explains:

In his personal individualism and bullish eccentricity, Churchill helped define the fight. It was an idea that was to lead him badly astray in the 1945 election, when he made the mistake of comparing Labour government bureaucrats to the Gestapo. But it was absolutely what was needed for the war.[221]

The idea of an emergency necessitating the acceptance of a leader and all his faults resurfaced in 2022, when some claimed that the Ukraine conflict obliged the retention of Johnson in office (at least for the time being) notwithstanding various objections to his conduct.[222] As his premiership came increasingly under threat, Johnson and his supporters defended him using the claim that he and his government had 'got the big calls right' in the critical areas of Brexit, the pandemic, and Ukraine.[223]

In executing the departures from norms to which he appeared to believe he was specially entitled, Johnson seemed capable of deeply cynical calculation, willing to mobilise the rawest of impulses, or at least displaying indifference as to whether his actions might have such an impact.[224] His earlier writing shows a full awareness of such tactics. Commenting on the 2002 French presidential election, in an article published in the *Daily Telegraph* on 25 April entitled 'Blunkett and Le Pen: what's the difference', Johnson commented on the approach to immigration and asylum being pursued by David Blunkett as Labour home secretary, who had, Johnson wrote:

yesterday talked about asylum seekers 'swamping' certain schools. He has not withdrawn the word, which – as he well knew – was once used by Mrs Thatcher, and which earned her the eternal obloquy of the Left. He has announced segregated education for immigrants; and he does so because he is respond-ing to the same set of public concerns that boosted Le Pen. Mr Blunkett is no fascist, merely an authoritar-ian. You may think he is quite right in his policies. But be in no doubt: he succeeds by playing to essentially the same gallery as Jean-Marie Le Pen.[225]

If such an interpretation was applicable to the Blair governments in the 2000s, then it would surely suit the Johnson administration just as well, for instance with its efforts to deport asylum seekers to Rwanda.[226] A willing-ness to pursue such tactics contributed to a number of the constitutional concerns we identify here. They include a variety of actual or at least arguable threats to objectivity in policymaking, adherence to international treaty com-mitments and human rights standards, the giving of due regard to the views of officials, and the promotion of well-informed, rational public debate.

Johnson also provided evidence that he might perceive even the direst of circumstances predominantly from the perspective of his own narrow self-interest. In his 2004 novel, *Seventy-Two Virgins*, Johnson depicted a prime minister who – confronted with a security threat in the

UK endangering among others the US president – is immediately concerned to ensure that he minimises possible damage to his own standing. One passage describes how the prime minister, sitting in COBRA (the Cabinet Office Briefing Rooms where the emergency committee of the same name convenes): 'the Prime Minister meditated not so much on the safety of the President or the crowd, but on the future of his government.'[227] Such an attitude, as Johnson conveys in the novel, can lead to a desire to evade accountability and to allow others – perhaps of less seniority – to carry risk. Johnson describes how:

the Prime Minister had instantly seen that these events could be fatal to his career. So there was one point he stressed in his brief conversation with [Deputy Assistant Commissioner Stephen] Purnell, namely that he, the Prime Minister, was taking political responsibility, of course, but no 'operational' responsibility. It would be quite wrong, the Prime Minister said, for him to second-guess the split-second decisions of the experts. That was why he, the Prime Minister, was going to leave such decisions to Purnell.[228]

Although arguably a satire, the novel gives a disconcertingly accurate insight into Johnson's own behaviour as prime minister. In response to the final Gray report on gatherings, for example, he both attested to his own responsibility while at the same time undermining its meaning.[229] The experience of this prolonged scandal suggested Johnson was never more tenacious than when defying pressure to resign. Indeed, the perceived insistence of previous prime ministers, faced with adversity, to avoid accountability and even resist removal from office, seems to have made an impression upon him. Johnson wrote in the *Daily Telegraph* on 29 January 2004 of Tony Blair's ability to retain office in the wake of scrutiny of matters related to the invasion of Iraq: 'he is a mixture of Harry Houdini and a greased piglet. He is barely human in his elusiveness. Nailing Blair is like trying to pin jelly to a wall.'[230] Writing in the same journal following the inconclusive general election of 2010, on 10 May Johnson described Gordon Brown as being 'like some illegal settler in the Sinai desert, lashing himself to the radiator, or like David Brent haunting *The Office* in that excruciating episode when he refuses to acknowledge that he has been sacked. Isn't there someone – the Queen's private secretary, the nice policeman on the door of Number 10 – whose job it is to tell him that the game is up?'[231] The question of how to oust a premier who is reluctant to leave can indeed be difficult to answer, as Johnson would demonstrate a little over a decade later.

A wider problem

The conduct of Johnson, explored further in the second part of this book, fits with the profile of a politician who felt exceptionally entitled to violate rules, regardless – or perhaps because – of the harm doing so might cause, and who sought to evade personal accountability for this kind of activity. For such an individual to occupy the post of prime minister is doubly a problem. They can cause difficulty directly through their own actions, and through contaminating the system around them. Johnson both tacitly and actively encouraged poor decisions and behaviour.[232] He thereby contributed to a deterioration of standards among ministers and officials, and the integrity of the political and constitutional system.[233] All who were within his governments, whether politicians or officials, were in some sense part of the Johnson enterprise for as long as they remained in post. Ministers at various points were required publicly to defend his actions – which they did with varying degrees of enthusiasm.[234]

But, as we have noted, he was not the whole of the problem. How, for instance, was the ascendancy of such a person possible? It was not for lack of knowledge of his flaws. For a long period prior to rising to the highest office, Johnson had openly promoted and acted upon various defects in his personal style. His unreliability was widely recognised (though it could be regarded in a light-hearted fashion).[235] His traits were known – and frowned upon – at the most senior level in the Conservative Party even before Johnson became an MP. In his memoir, the Conservative politician Andrew Mitchell recalls once having responsibility within the party for the process of identifying potential electoral candidates. In 1993, while Mitchell held this role, Johnson first appeared on the list, despite resistance (as well as support), including from Conservative members of the European Parliament. The Conservative prime minister at the time, John Major – so an intermediary informed Mitchell – had an intense dislike of Johnson for the nature of his journalistic coverage of the European integration project (which had by this point become a highly sensitive subject within the party). Major summoned Mitchell to see him at his House of Commons office. The prime minister, Mitchell recalls, greeted him in the following terms: 'Ah, Andrew, thanks for coming: what the fuck do you mean by putting Boris Johnson on the candidates list?'[236]

Negative views of Johnson, including among those who had worked closely with him, persisted over the decades. They cannot have been improved by incidents such as Johnson's being removed from the Conservative frontbench in 2004 over aspects of his personal life that had attracted media attention and – specifically – accounts he had given of them. The then leader of the opposition, Lord (Michael) Howard of Lympne, recalled in 2019 that: 'my Director of Communications at the time was convinced that Boris had lied to him, and strongly advised me that I should take the action which I took.'[237] In 2016, Johnson's hopes of becoming Conservative leader (and thereby prime minister) in the forthcoming party contest were ended when his supposed ally, Gove, announced a candidacy of his own, stating that 'Boris cannot provide the leadership or build the team for the task ahead.'[238] In a diary entry for 24 September 2017, the Conservative MP Alan Duncan offered an assessment of Johnson, then the secretary of state at the Foreign Office, where Duncan was a minister of state. Johnson, Duncan held:

has a self-deluding mock-romantic passion which is not rooted in realism. He is disloyal. A decade of press attention has gone to his head ... I have lost any respect for him. He is a clown, a self-centred ego, an embarrassing buffoon, with an untidy mind and sub-zero diplomatic judgment. He is an international stain on our reputation. He is a lonely, selfish, ill-disciplined, shambolic, shameless clot. Grrr.[239]

But as we know, manifest personal flaws did not prevent the Johnson ascendancy, and may well have assisted it. Various groups – senior Conservatives, party members, and then voters – were willing to endorse him in sufficient numbers to facilitate and secure his rise, and significant sections of the media proved remarkably supportive until relatively close to the end – or even beyond it.[240] In 2019, for example, notwithstanding his earlier reservations, Gove was willing to serve in a Johnson government. Conservative colleagues in the House of Commons often proved compliant in voting for dubious legislative proposals, and were for some time surprisingly tolerant of his transgressions.[241] It is worth asking why those who had reservations were able to overcome them, or at least did not act upon them in a way that successfully denied Johnson, or removed him from, high office prior to the revolt of July 2022. A central factor was his perceived potential electoral appeal – of particular importance in 2019 when he was first installed at Number 10.[242] In narrow terms, the December 2019 general election victory seemed to prove that the gamble of elevating Johnson to the premiership had been a success, providing him with a degree of political insulation when difficulties later began to multiply. In such circumstances, given a considerable degree of discretion to manifest his own weaknesses, Johnson's character became a capital 'C' Constitutional Question in its own right.

But how Johnson had even reached a position where he could be regarded as a viable leadership candidate in 2019, and why the party was able to make such a reckless decision, still requires further explanation. Again, it is worth considering the perceptions of some of those who were close to him. Johnson and his family were firmly entrenched in senior Conservative circles for many years, for instance from his time at Oxford.[243] People within such networks might be to some extent aware of his faults, but could also be sentimental about or admiring of him.[244] They might choose to allow him the benefit of the doubt. In a diary entry for 19 June 2019, faced with the prospect of a Johnson leadership and premiership, Sasha Swire, wife of Conservative MP Hugo Swire, may have captured the doubts of many in the party when she wrote:

> I don't sleep all night. The absolute fear of letting the Blond and his mistress, and his whole Kardashian family, elbowing each other out of the way to get into the limelight, into No.10 has brought on a bout of political melancholia. H and I, like everyone else, will now be shutting our eyes and holding our noses as we put our crosses in Boris's box. Because, really, no one knows which Boris we are getting: the clown, the journalist, the adulterer and liar, the sensitive one, the big-mouth one, the messy one, the clever one…What we won't be getting is someone who is manageable or trainable; Boris likes to shake things up, break the rules, take the speeding fine then speed again.[245]

As someone who was far from being a Johnson devotee, Swire then made a distinction through which she provided a clue as to how those within the Conservative Party who were well aware of his flaws might decide to accommodate themselves with his advancement, and perhaps conventions of public life; and on self-restraint by the powerful.

If any of that delicate balance goes astray – as it has – as it *is* – our democracy is undermined. Our government is culpable, in small but important ways, of failing to honour these conventions.[196]

Characteristics of Boris Johnson

In their speeches both of these critics made specific reference to the prime minister. Any consideration of problems of the type they identified in relation to the Johnson administration must take into account the person whose name it bears. According to long-established constitutional principle, at its highest level, the UK government is a collective endeavour. It is about more than any one individual, regardless of how vivid a character they might be. Cabinet is made up of more than twenty senior departmental ministers each bringing their own qualities, strengths, weaknesses, connections, and ambitions to their role. The most prominent among them can possess more 'hard' powers – such as responsibility for budgets and statutory authorities – than the premier who appointed them.[197] Nonetheless, prime ministers are crucially important.

The system of government is geared to respond and shape itself partly in response to the way in which each tolerate his failings longer than they should have done. Swire advanced the idea of there being two Johnsons:

> Good Boris likes getting rid of regulations, spy satellites (well, that figures, with all his shagging around), rights-first culture and reverse discrimination. Good Boris laughs at pomposity and grandiosity ... He will be ... tolerant of people's foibles and weaknesses. But bad Boris, the Boris we fear, is the casual one, the one that can't be bothered to read spreadsheets, the one that misses deadlines, the one that makes everything into a joke, the one that trusts everyone and no one. We wait with bated breath...[246]

Such thinking was problematic in two senses. First, it is unrealistic to suppose that, over a period in office, a politician will only exhibit their supposed strengths and not any weaknesses they possess. Second, what Swire identified as traits of the 'good Boris' could easily be seen as different ways of describing the 'bad Boris'. Some of the worst defects of the Johnson premiership involved those characteristics Swire might have held to be his 'good' features, such as showing disdain for regulations. Indeed, his being 'tolerant of people's foibles and weaknesses' was a running source of problems and might have been the immediate cause of his downfall, in regard to the Chris Pincher case. What one person might regard as 'foibles and weaknesses' might better be viewed as extremely problematic patterns of behaviour that should rule someone out of the holding of public office.

Duncan, a politician who was – as we have seen – brutal in his assessment of Johnson, committed another (common) error that perhaps helps explain how Johnson was able to ascend despite his capacity to appal. It may be that the very implausibility of his upward career trajectory encouraged a mistaken assumption that it had reached its limits among those who might otherwise have taken firmer steps to resist him. Such a seemingly unlikely phenomenon as Johnson attaining high office of any kind was perhaps difficult to understand within the context of more conventional political perception, and therefore harder to resist. Certainly Duncan, like others at various points, thought that Johnson's moment had passed in September 2017, writing that:

> he doesn't appreciate that the gloss has gone. His comedy routine has gone stale; his lack of seriousness in a serious job rankles; and he has little following among MPs. Most activists, even if still amused by his buffoonery, no longer see him as a credible prime minister. He seems to have embarked on a reckless journey into oblivion.[247]

Duncan was not the first to mistakenly discount Johnson's future prospects.[248] For example, one press article written immediately after his 2004 removal from the opposition frontbench concluded: 'the episode brings an end to an unlikely but uniquely engaging political career.'[249] Less than two years after Duncan made his September 2017 journal entry, Johnson was prime minister. Another diarist, Lionel Barber, former editor of the *Financial Times*, recorded on 24 July 2019 that:

> I still find it hard to believe that Boris Johnson has made it to Downing Street. He was an agreeable buffoon in Brussels as the *Daily Telegraph* correspondent, though adept at hiding his ambition. Maybe that's why we never took him seriously, even when he was mayor of London. *Big mistake.*[250]

That the political system and those operating within it enabled Johnson is suggestive of a wider problem. A similar observation might be made when we consider some of the objectionable constitutional policies with which his administration was associated. This programme had an ideological aspect to it, with a populist flavour, positing a scenario in which various elite institutions that sought to frustrate the will of the people must now face a reckoning. An expression of this position came in the 2019 Conservative general election manifesto which claimed that:

> The failure of Parliament to deliver Brexit – the way so many MPs have devoted themselves to thwarting

the democratic decision of the British people in the 2016 referendum – has opened up a destabilising and potentially extremely damaging rift between politicians and people.

Having constructed this supposed problem, the party alluded to a programme that seemed likely to entail a weakening of the restraints on the executive that Parliament and the courts provide:

After Brexit we ... need to look at the broader aspects of our constitution: the relationship between the Government, Parliament and the courts; the functioning of the Royal Prerogative; the role of the House of Lords; and access to justice for ordinary people ... We will update the Human Rights Act and administrative law to ensure that there is a proper balance between the rights of individuals, our vital national security and effective government. We will ensure that judicial review is available to protect the rights of the individuals against an overbearing state, while ensuring that it is not abused to conduct politics by another means or to create needless delays.[251]

This position reflected in part what has become, over a period of more than a decade, a powerful strand of thought within the Conservative Party. It can be seen to a significant extent as connected to, and an extension of, Brexit, both as an agenda and a political experience. Leaving the EU entailed an abrupt break in constitutional continuity, and many of those most committed to it came to perceive the various institutions and norms of the system as hindrances. On 27 March 2019, the Conservative MP Steve Baker spoke to the radically pro-Brexit European Research Group (ERG), of which he was a leading member (the text is reproduced in a book by his Conservative ally, Mark Francois MP). Expressing his opposition to the EU exit agreement that Theresa May was about to present to Parliament for a third time, Baker exhibited a destructive attitude. He described himself as:

> consumed by a ferocious rage ... Like all of you, I have wrestled with my conscience, with the evidence before me, with the text of the Treaty, and I resolved that I would vote against this deal however often it was presented, come what may, if it meant the fall of the Government and the destruction of the Conservative Party.
>
> By God, right now, if I think of the worthless, ignorant cowards and knaves in the House today, voting for things they do not understand, which would surrender our right to govern ourselves, I would tear this building down and bulldoze the rubble into the river. God help me, I would.
>
> But I know that if we do this, if we insist and we

take this all the way, we might find ourselves standing in the rubble of our Party and our constitution
and our Government and our country. I am so filled
with rage that we should have been deliberately put
in this place by people whose addiction to power
without accountability has led them to place before
this country a choice between Remain or Brexit in
Name Only.

I want to destroy, to tear down, to break. I confess
to you I do not know what to do.[252]

Using similarly troubling language, in a July 2022 BBC
interview Baker asserted his potential suitability for the
role of prime minister, discussing how he would operate
in the event that – in his words – 'I seize power'.[253] The
ERG – and the ongoing tendency within the Conservative Party it signifies – was an influential force. While it
was instrumental in placing Johnson in the premiership,
it did so as a means of pursuing the shared objectives of its
members. It was not a Johnson faction as such, and Baker
became in 2022 one of the most prominent and relatively
early advocates of the resignation of the premier.[254] While
Baker was a backbencher under Johnson, some of his
most hard-line allies found their way into the Cabinet.[255]
Indeed, the desire to overturn constitutional norms had
significant representation at this highest level. Dominic
Raab MP, for instance, after serving as foreign secretary,
was – from 2021 – secretary of state for justice and lord

chancellor. He was a longstanding critic of the way in which the courts uphold rights, and set about pursuing aspects of his agenda.[256]

The constitutional programme of the Johnson governments, then, was more than a product of Johnson himself. His departure might entail the disappearance of some of the aspects he contributed personally and the influences he channelled. But the entire agenda will not necessarily vanish. His successor at Number 10 may wish or feel pressured to maintain at least parts of it. Furthermore, his behaviour and the failure to restrain it in its various manifestations revealed weaknesses in the UK constitution. That it struggled to contain Johnson and the various forces associated with him may be less an indicator of his uniqueness than of the system itself being vulnerable. While the circumstances of the Johnson episode may not precisely replicate themselves, features of them could recur. They need not necessarily even involve a Conservative government. The problem is greater than any one politician or party. For this reason, measures for the reinforcement of constitutional standards and rules need careful consideration. We approach this task later in the book. As a preparatory step to this task, we now consider in more detail the difficulties that developed.

Part Two

The Problem in Detail

We argue in this work that recent and probably ongoing developments at UK government level give clear cause for concern about the robustness of the constitution. In this part of the book we offer a closer analysis of aspects of the problem. While we supply a degree of detail, we are necessarily selective, providing examples that illustrate broader patterns. We discuss a spectrum of activities, diverse in scope and all of them important in their own right. They range from actions that may not specifically transgress any rule but nonetheless are objectionable, through to clearer departures from constitutional conventions, and finally unlawful and illegal activities. We consider possible violations of treaty commitments and international law, and threats to human rights and the rule of law. The Johnson governments undermined various public institutions and the values associated with them. Participants in them, furthermore, showed disregard for the mechanisms intended to ensure their compliance with constitutional standards, and the administration sought to remove some of those constraints to which it is subject.

Troubling activities not specifically transgressing any clear constitutional rule

As already discussed, the functioning of any system assumes to some extent that participants within it will adhere to certain standards of conduct. It is possible that someone might behave in a way that is detrimental to the proper functioning of the political system, and that perhaps departs from basic social norms, without actually violating a clearly defined constitutional rule (of a hard legal form or otherwise). For example, the quality of public discourse – how far it allows for the rational, measured, good-natured interchange of ideas, and seeks to establish and adhere to an agreed body of factual information – is crucial to democracy.[1] The way in which a public figure engages in debate can have beneficial or detrimental consequences in this regard.

By the time Johnson became prime minister he already had a regrettable record, which he maintained thereafter. One negative aspect of his interventions has been a tendency to draw crass comparisons that do more to demean than illuminate their subjects. A recurring target in his dubious employment of this rhetorical tactic has been the EU. In a 2007 work, for instance, Johnson compared the contemporary European integration project to the Roman Empire.[2] Perhaps the most unpleasant analogy he has attempted to draw was between the EU and the Third Reich. His 2014 work on Churchill describes the Nazi plan to transform a conquered continent into, as Johnson put it, 'a sinister edition of the European Union'. The Reich minister of economics, Walther Funk, produced a scheme for what Johnson labelled 'a European common market ... a single currency, a central bank, a common agricultural policy, and other familiar ideas'. Johnson went on to refer to the prospect of a 'Gestapo-controlled Nazi EU' in which 'the authorities would have been free to pursue their hateful racist ideology'.[3]

What makes for low-quality journalism and history becomes even more objectionable in the mouth of a senior representative of the UK. As foreign secretary, Johnson made a comment appearing to liken the French government and EU to guards in a Nazi prisoner of war camp.[4] Such comparisons are a grotesque misrepresentation of the EU and a deep insult to the member states (of which the UK was one until 2020) that comprise it. Perhaps even worse, they serve to belittle the suffering inflicted by one of the most despicable regimes in human history. A responsible politician, committed to values set out in the *Seven Principles of Public Life*, would not seek to exploit these events for the sake of a cheap gibe – one intended, moreover, to be at the cost of longstanding and vital allies. As prime minister, Johnson persisted in this lamentable habit, for example when claiming parallels between Brexit and the armed struggle of Ukraine against Russian invasion in 2022.[5]

Possibly the most immediately damaging case of dishonest and irresponsible messaging involving Johnson and others in his governments relates to the Northern Ireland Protocol. It formed a crucial part of the EU Withdrawal Agreement that Johnson, his administration, and his party presented to the electorate as a great diplomatic success in 2019.[6] Johnson insisted in public, falsely, that the Protocol would not entail any checks on goods moving from Great Britain to Northern Ireland.[7] Yet there is evidence that, around the same time, senior figures within the UK government were privately reassuring those whose support or acquiescence was wanted and who might dislike the Protocol that the UK administration was not firmly committed to it.[8] The UK government, moreover, soon became increasingly explicit in their opposition to the Protocol, criticising and undermining the operation of the agreement. This approach manifested itself in various ways, such as being obstructive over measures necessary for the implementation of the Protocol,[9] and unilaterally declining to introduce aspects of it.[10] The government threatened more severe breaks with the Protocol,[11] introducing bills to Parliament designed to give it the power to do so.[12] While engaging in such tactics, the UK administration insisted on blaming the EU for problems – supposed or actual – with the Protocol.[13] The UK government has magnified its dishonesty by presenting itself as setting out to safeguard the peace process, which – in this questionable version of events – the EU is risking by expecting the Protocol to be honoured.[14] Making a success of the Protocol was always likely to prove a challenging task. This dishonest behaviour has surely made it more difficult and helped destabilise a territory within the UK itself that has been the site of violent conflict, the return of which cannot be entirely excluded.[15]

A further requirement for the healthy functioning of the UK constitution, the practical realisation of which is difficult precisely to set out, involves the departure of senior politicians from their posts. Ministers should be able to recognise when it is time for them to leave, and that to do otherwise is to place their personal interest over the public interest. If they fail to act as they should, then others need to prevail upon them to do so. The Johnson era has arguably been marked by a particular tenacity on the part of political office holders. Priti Patel, for instance, held firm despite the adviser on ministers' interests concluding she had violated the *Ministerial Code* by bullying officials. Johnson, far from forcing an exit from government upon Patel, firmly supported his home secretary and disagreed with the findings of the adviser, who resigned.[16] Johnson himself, along with Rishi Sunak (the latter, it seems, reluctantly, the former not) stayed on despite being subject to criminal sanctions in relation to social distancing laws.[17] That they did so was remarkable but did not represent a departure from a defined rule. The lack of a clear precedent for their position might have been a problem for them in one sense, but it also meant that there was no previous example to point to of a resignation taking place in such circumstances. Though Johnson was eventually forced out of office by ministers and MPs of his own party, the immediate cause was not the fixed penalty notice or his overall handling of the episode involving lockdown gatherings (though it was for reasons that were certainly serious). The worrying conclusion is that a senior minister found to have committed a crime in future might feel able to point to the Johnson–Sunak precedent both to downplay the significance of their transgression, and to assert that it is proper for them to continue in post.

Sunak has furnished another example of conduct that could seem questionable even if it was not prohibited: that he – not only as an MP but also as chancellor of the exchequer – held a US green card.[18] In this particular instance – and perhaps others – it may be that the reason for the absence of an express prohibition on a given behaviour was that it had never occurred to previous rule-makers that someone who held high office would engage in it. One of the functions of the *Ministerial Code* has been, through the updating process, to capture transgressions that have been exposed since the previous edition appeared, and include wording intended to rule out their reoccurrence.[19] However, the 2022 *Ministerial Code* does not appear to have taken the opportunity to clarify the position in this area. Perhaps the reason was that to do so would be to admit fault, which the government seemed to be reluctant to do. Another example of a decision that – though apparently within defined rules – was constitutionally questionable was the insistence of Johnson on appointing Dominic Cummings as his senior special adviser upon becoming prime minister in July 2019, despite Cummings having been found in contempt of Parliament in March of that year.[20]

Departures from more clearly defined rules

We can also find significant examples of departures from rules that lack direct legal force but are more clearly defined. As noted above, communications that are constitutionally problematic may not directly violate a specific rule, and as such proscription may be difficult to apply. However, some ways in which the government went about messaging can be more clearly established to amount to a transgression of norms. The UK Statistics Authority, with a statutory basis in the Statistics and Registration Services Act 2007, has functions that include 'publicly challenging the misuse of statistics'.[21] In performing its tasks, the Authority had cause to query the way in which the Johnson governments handled the presentation of official figures. For instance, in February 2022, the Authority identified misleading accounts of crime measurements by Johnson and the Home Office.[22]

In assessing the possibility of clearly identified departures from rules that do not necessarily amount to violations of the law, it is useful to consider texts to which the government is in theory committed, and for the drafting of which it was and is responsible. We have already measured performance against *The Cabinet Manual*. A more live document, subject to regular re-issues, is the *Ministerial Code*.[23] The prime minister, supported by the Cabinet secretary, is responsible for issuing it, for any alterations to its content, and ultimately for interpreting and enforcing it.[24] Johnson already issued two versions, in 2019 and 2022. Much public scrutiny of Johnson and his adherence or otherwise to standards has focused on the *Ministerial Code*. The following table identifies some problematic areas in relation to rules drawn from just one section of the code (albeit one of primary importance). It assumes that the text applies to the prime minister as well as other ministers.

Possible violations of rules set out in the Ministerial Code, *section 1, 'Ministers of the Crown' (cited text in italics)*

Cited text	Examples of questionable activity
1.1 Ministers of the Crown are expected to maintain high standards of behaviour and to behave in a way that upholds the highest standards of propriety.	• Obvious examples of failure to meet this requirement were exposed by the police and Sue Gray investigations into gatherings in government buildings during a time of Covid restrictions.[25]
1.2 Ministers should be professional in all their dealings and treat all those with whom they come into contact with consideration and respect. Working relationships, including with civil servants, ministerial and parliamentary colleagues and parliamentary staff should be proper and appropriate. Harassing, bullying or other inappropriate or discriminating behaviour wherever it takes place is not consistent with the Ministerial Code and will not be tolerated.	• The independent adviser on ministers' interests, at the time Sir Alex Allan, found the home secretary, Priti Patel, to have fallen short in this area, though Johnson did not accept this view; this was followed by the resignation of Allan in November 2020.[26] • Johnson failed properly to take into account existing concerns about Chris Pincher.[27]
1.3 The Ministerial Code should be read against the background of the overarching duty on Ministers to comply with the law and to protect the integrity of public life. They are expected to observe the Seven Principles of Public Life, set out at Annex A, and the following principles of Ministerial conduct...	• The attempted prorogation of 2019 was found to be unlawful. • Both the prime minister and the chancellor of the exchequer, along with numerous officials, violated criminal law through their involvement in lockdown gatherings.[28] • Johnson behaved in a way that seemed to lead to successive holders of the post of independent adviser on ministers' interests to resign: Allan in November 2020, then Lord (Christopher) Geidt in June 2022.[29] Johnson thereby demonstrated lack of due respect for mechanisms for the protection of integrity in public life.

Cited text	Examples of questionable activity
	• For adherence to the *Seven Principles of Public Life*, see p. 17. • With regards to international law and treaty obligations – if they come within 'the law' as employed in this passage – there were serious issues involving, in particular, refugee policy and the Northern Ireland Protocol.[30] • The government set out in various ways to pursue programmes that might serve to lessen possible legal restrictions upon its conduct, for instance through its plans to change the way in which human rights are protected.[31] It was reluctant to accept proposals to enhance the promotion of integrity in public life.[32] Indeed, the Johnson administration actively pursued courses of action likely to weaken mechanisms intended for such purposes, for instance through undermining the powers and independence from the UK government of the Electoral Commission.[33]
a. The principle of collective responsibility applies to all Government Ministers;	• One implication of the principle described in this paragraph is that those ministers serving in the government were, for so long as they remained in their posts, party to the abuses perpetrated by Johnson and others, even if they were not directly involved in them. There were points before July 2022 at which they could and perhaps should have chosen to resign (for instance, when the police issued multiple fixed penalty notices, including to Johnson and Sunak, over lockdown gatherings). • The drive from within his own party to finally oust Johnson that occurred in July 2022 involved a collapse in collective responsibility, with ministers publicly calling on Johnson to resign while remaining in their posts.[34]

Cited text	Examples of questionable activity
b. Ministers have a duty to Parliament to account, and be held to account, for the policies, decisions and actions of their departments and agencies;	• Ministers have shown, under pressure, a tendency to displace blame to officials, in contradiction of basic constitutional principle.[35]
c. It is of paramount importance that Ministers give accurate and truthful information to Parliament, correcting any inadvertent error at the earliest opportunity. Ministers who knowingly mislead Parliament will be expected to offer their resignation to the Prime Minister;	• Ministers, including the prime minister, seem to have provided inaccurate information to Parliament on numerous occasions, and their performance in correcting the record when challenged has been questioned.[36] In April 2022, Johnson was made subject to an inquiry by the Commons Privileges Committee into whether assertions he had made to the Commons regarding lockdown gatherings amounted to a contempt of the House.[37]
d. Ministers should be as open as possible with Parliament and the public, refusing to provide information only when disclosure would not be in the public interest, which should be decided in accordance with the relevant statutes and the Freedom of Information Act 2000…	• The government was resistant regarding the publication of details about procurement processes during the pandemic, acting unlawfully.[38] • In arguing that its Northern Ireland Protocol Bill, introduced in June 2022, was compatible with international law, the government failed to explain the underlying justifications it might have for this claim.[39]
f. Ministers must ensure that no conflict arises, or appears to arise, between their public duties and their private interests;	• The means by which Johnson arranged financial assistance for the renovation of the Downing Street flat was a source of doubts about compliance in this area. The investigation by the adviser raised concerns, but did not conclude that rules had been broken.[40]
g. Ministers should not accept any gift or hospitality which might, or might reasonably appear to, compromise their judgement or place them under an improper obligation;	• See immediately above. While the adviser did not find Johnson to have broken the rules, the concerns he raised with respect to the renovation and the way it was funded are relevant to this stipulation.

Cited text	Examples of questionable activity
h. Ministers in the House of Commons must keep separate their roles as Minister and constituency Member;	• Decisions over the allocation of financial support for 'levelling up' purposes have been questioned, with claims about the constituencies of Cabinet members being notable beneficiaries.[41]
i. Ministers must not use government resources for Party political purposes...	• There is reasonable cause for concern over the handling of procurement processes during the pandemic, and for potential conflicts of interest not being satisfactorily addressed.[42] • Allegations about the improper targeting of 'levelling up' funds have included the claim that they are used as a means of disciplining Conservative backbenchers in parliamentary votes.[43]
j. Ministers must uphold the political impartiality of the Civil Service and not ask civil servants to act in any way which would conflict with the Civil Service Code as set out in the Constitutional Reform and Governance Act 2010.	• Departure of senior officials on an unprecedented scale arguably presented challenges to the meaningful maintenance of Whitehall impartiality and other Civil Service values such as objectivity.[44]

Violation of law

Our discussion so far conveys the impression of a government that could be indifferent to the possibility of its actions serving to test or abrogate established constitutional understandings, and that at times appeared actively to seek such outcomes. We have considered the impact of this approach in the sphere of rules and expectations, more or less clearly defined, that might not be fully underpinned by – for instance – statute, but that are nonetheless fundamental to the functioning of the democratic system. This general pattern has spilled over into the realms of domestic and international law, within which transgressions can be easier to identify with precision. As with other aspects of the phenomenon identified in this work, while many influences are involved, the problematic person at the centre of the government was – in this case literally – a prominent offender. We have already discussed how Johnson gave clear signals of what his constitutional approach as prime minister might be long before he came to the post. His own attitudes, or perhaps those of the persona he projected (the distinctions between which are difficult precisely to draw), seem to have inclined him towards casualness and even active contempt regarding not only softer norms but also law in its various forms.

To underscore this point, it is worth returning to some of his prior journalistic output. It suggests an author who disliked feeling constrained by rules, even if he (grudgingly) accepted they were objectively justified, or at least difficult to argue against. His longstanding tendency – previously discussed – to become involved in various controversies suggests a habit of acting upon this disposition. Seeking to present this quality as a virtue, Johnson presumably judged it to be a source of potential appeal to his audience. His ascendancy suggests that he may well have been correct in this assessment, and political success probably reinforced this view on his part, encouraging him to continue to associate with and act upon this philosophy. Mr Toads tend not to obey highway codes.

The rules to which Johnson objected could include laws. In his introduction to a 2007 collection *Life in the Fast Lane: The Johnson Guide to Cars*, in familiar hyperbolic mode, he celebrated the automobile as a major contributor to 'human freedom', that in his view the 'state' was inevitably prone to restricting.[45] Complaining about road safety measures, such as those pursued by 'the Liberal Democrats of Islington', Johnson described speed cameras as 'Orwellian', and held that various 'lobby groups', 'lawyers', 'politicians', and 'newspapers' all had vested interests prompting their calls for new regulations. Consequently, Johnson went on:

> in the face of ... overwhelming pressure it is all but insane for anyone to object, even when the safety measure in question is manifestly pointless and anti-democratic. I will not now make a fuss about the ban on mobiles in cars, since I don't think I could win a statistical shoot-out with the 'elf 'n' safety boys ... Nor will I object to seat belts, since they plainly save lives, though my grandfather never wore one in his life.

While conceding 'that the Johnson family has been pretty religious about the use of children's car seats', the future prime minister asked rhetorically 'what about booster seats? ... When we were children we didn't have car seats. We didn't even have seat belts ... we all felt pretty happy and safe.'[46]

In this passage Johnson displayed a propensity to dislike and challenge laws intended to promote public safety. Even while conceding that he was unable to refute their scientific justification, Johnson was nonetheless determined to continue to question their legitimacy through employing empty anecdotes and claims about people feeling secure without the regulations. The libertarian political packaging in which he wrapped this wilful ignorance was flimsy, and the attempt to invoke Orwell, who was concerned with genuine infringements on human freedom, rather than those of which Johnson complained, was dubious.

The idea of someone who was willing to promote such views holding high office is concerning from the standpoint of objective, evidence-based policymaking, the principles of which appear in various constitutional documents cited in this book. For that person to be prime minister during a global pandemic is closer to calamitous. We cannot yet achieve clarity on how far and in what way Johnson sought to battle with what he might have regarded as the Whitehall "elf 'n' safety boys' over the Covid response, and what the consequences were. The inquiry into the handling of this emergency will perhaps be revealing in this sense. But we can be certain in another sense. Whatever attitude Johnson had towards them, and regardless of whether his approach served to delay or alter them in substantial and problematic ways, his government introduced major legal restrictions designed to protect public health. Johnson may have been willing to see such regulations come into force and to promote adherence to them. But – in confirmation of his unwillingness to place public interest above personal gratification – he broke this law.

Johnson and his supporters sought to present him almost as a bystander unwittingly drawn into events.[47] But the Sue Gray report, with its references to failings of political leadership, suggests a different view is possible, and that it is hard to depict Johnson merely as a marginal figure in the criminal activities that occurred in a building that was his home and office. The desire to hold parties, regardless of the possibly severe consequences, certainly seems to have seized the Number 10 Downing Street presided over by Johnson. This habit and the criminality connected to it have probably attracted the most attention of any of the constitutionally problematic aspects of his government. But other violations of law took place, involving unlawful as opposed to illegal activity, when the government lost judicial reviews. That a government in a particular state *can* be restrained in this way is an indicator of democratic wellbeing. Nonetheless, the Johnson administration was involved in various high-profile cases that arose from or revealed aspects of its tendency to depart from norms and standards in ways and to extents that were worrisome. Furthermore, its response to efforts to hold it to account in this way – as we will discuss here and below – deliberately conveyed less than full respect for the vital process of judicial review, and the people, institutions, and processes associated with it. Moreover, the government appeared intent upon loosening legal restraints upon it.

The most dramatic government defeat in a judicial review of the Johnson premiership came when the Supreme Court, in September 2019, ruled the attempted prorogation of Parliament as unlawful. The reasoning was that the measure would represent an affront to the constitutional position of Parliament, a crucial aspect of which was the function of holding government to account.[48] That the Johnson administration had to be taken to court to prevent it from suppressing Parliament, and that members and allies of it should respond in a less than gracious way to the outcome of the case, reflected poorly upon them.[49] This episode demonstrated the importance of the courts as potentially a final defence against democratic abuse, and the dangers associated with any attempt to circumscribe their influence. Further significant litigation involved practices in the award of government contracts in relation to the pandemic. It has revealed questionable practices such as the bypassing of normal procedures, perhaps in ways and to an extent that the (undeniably grave) circumstances of the time did not require,[50] and a lack of transparency about the details of contracts.[51] Partly because of the scale of the sums of money involved, these revelations were considerable grounds for concern.[52]

We have discussed the significance of the confirmed breaking of criminal law by both a sitting prime minister and chancellor of the exchequer, and the fact that both persisted in office regardless. The criminality involved extended far beyond these two senior members of the government, taking in various officials. In total, eighty-three people received between them 126 fixed-penalty notices.[53] This scale of infringement was suggestive of a more general laxity of approach, among senior civil servants as well as politicians. How far could such a culture be expected to sustain constitutional values, particularly given the extent of their dependence upon voluntary compliance and commitment to good behaviour?

A further dubious distinction for the Johnson premiership was its willingness to disparage treaty commitments; to toy publicly with courses of action that could call them into question or directly violate them; and to actually engage in such policies. Previous UK administrations have behaved in ways that have been controversial from the perspective of international law – for instance, the participation of Tony Blair's Labour government in the invasion of Iraq of 2003.[54] Nonetheless, under the Johnson governments such conduct became habitual and almost an ideological approach in its own right. On at least one occasion the government openly admitted that a plan to

create the power to override the Northern Ireland Protocol would put it in violation of international law (though
it attempted more recently to claim that a similar scheme
does not amount to such a transgression).[55] The following exchanges in the House of Commons involving the
then secretary of state for Northern Ireland, Brandon
Lewis, date from 8 September 2020. They help illustrate
the cross-party controversy that the proposal (included
in the Internal Market Bill 2020 but removed successfully
by the House of Lords) generated. The contributions confirmed, moreover, the tendency for a close link between
the transgression of norms (enough of a problem in itself)
and negative substantive consequences.

Mrs Theresa May
(Maidenhead) (Con)

The United Kingdom Government signed the withdrawal agreement with the Northern Ireland protocol.
This Parliament voted that withdrawal agreement into
UK legislation. The Government are now changing
the operation of that agreement. Given that, how
can the Government reassure future international
partners that the UK can be trusted to abide by the
legal obligations in the agreements it signs?...

Sir Robert Neill
(Bromley and Chislehurst) (Con)

The Secretary of State has said that he and the Government are committed to the rule of law. Does he recognise that adherence to the rule of law is not negotiable? Against that background, will he assure us that nothing that is proposed in this legislation does, or potentially might, breach international legal obligations or international legal arrangements that we have entered into?...

Brandon Lewis
(Great Yarmouth) (Con)

I would say to my hon. Friend that yes, this does break international law in a very specific and limited way. We are taking the power to disapply the EU law concept of direct effect, required by article 4, in certain very tightly defined circumstances. There are clear precedents of this for the UK and, indeed, other countries needing to consider their international obligations as circumstances change. I say to hon. Members here, many of whom would have been in this House when we passed the Finance Act 2013, that that Act contains an example of treaty override. It contains provisions that expressly disapply international tax treaties to the extent that these conflict with the general anti-abuse rule. I say to my hon. Friend that we are determined to ensure that we

are delivering on the agreement that we have in the protocol, and our leading priority is to do that through the
negotiations and through the Joint Committee work.
The clauses that will be in the Bill tomorrow are specifically there should that fail, ensuring that we can deliver
on our commitment to the people of Northern Ireland.

Andrew Gwynne
(Denton and Reddish) (Lab)

I am astounded that the Secretary of State has just
conceded that he is proposing to break international
law. Perhaps for the first time I agree with the right
hon. Member for Maidenhead (Mrs May). It is a question of trust when it comes to signing international
treaties. We cannot condemn others for seemingly
breaking the international rules-based order if we are
prepared to do the same. It is incredibly damaging to
our reputation if we are seeking to acquire trade treaties and the UK internal market Bill tomorrow seeks
to disapply section 7A of the European Union (Withdrawal) Act 2018.[56]

Undermining public institutions and
the values associated with them

Benjamin Disraeli proclaimed in a public speech in April 1872 that 'the programme of the Conservative party is to maintain the Constitution of the country'. His electoral objective – followed by subsequent Conservative leaders – was to achieve and maintain a support base that cut across social classes. A central way in which he sought to attain this goal was through promoting loyalty to entities such as the monarchy, the House of Lords, the Established Church, and the Union. Disraeli also depicted an enemy, referring in a talk given the following June to 'a body of public men' influenced by 'the philosophy and politics of the Continent' committed to 'Liberalism' and 'cosmopolitan' values. He claimed that this group sought to substitute these 'cosmopolitan for national principles'. Through this rhetorical tactic, Disraeli intended to create and aggravate divisions among opponents, and to acquire some of the Liberals' supporters. The purpose of these Liberal cosmopolitans, Disraeli asserted, was 'to attack the institutions of the country under the name of Reform, and to make war on the manners and customs of the people of this country under the pretext of Progress'. Depictions of this 'body of public men' of the nineteenth century are similar to contemporary caricatures of remainers, 'lefty lawyers', and representatives of various causes connected to the so-called 'culture wars'. Johnson employed them

THE PROBLEM IN DETAIL

for similar purposes to Disraeli. But rather than seeking to rally actual and potential supporters in defence of institutions, the Johnson governments were prone consciously to making them a target. In the scenario now being posited in and around the Conservative Party, malign forces have infiltrated and achieved hegemony within established social institutions. The immediate objective seems less to be to protect these entities against cosmopolitan, continentally inspired liberalism, and more to undermine and exert stronger influence over them.[57] The following table lists some key institutions and provides examples (drawing on episodes and tendencies already discussed in this work and other material) of the challenges they faced during the Johnson premiership.

Institution	Examples of challenges faced during the Johnson premiership
Parliament as a whole	• Unlawful attempt to prorogue Parliament in 2019. • Increasing emphasis on the use of delegated legislation, reducing the extent of parliamentary involvement in the law-making process, and in oversight of the executive.
House of Commons	• Johnson and other ministers making seemingly misleading statements – intentionally or otherwise – to the House.
House of Lords	• Efforts by the government at legislative 'ping pong' stage to minimise the opportunity of the Lords to resist constitutionally controversial measures.[58] • There has been criticism of the volume of appointments made to the Lords under Johnson, and questions raised about certain individuals chosen.[59]

Institution	Examples of challenges faced during the Johnson premiership
Devolved institutions	• A relative concentration of powers at UK level post-Brexit, arguably to the detriment of the devolved tier. • In Northern Ireland, the behaviour of the UK government with respect to the Protocol has added to tensions in a scenario in which the viability of devolution has again come into question.
The judiciary	• Made subject to political pressure, with the possibility looming of legal restrictions on its ability to conduct judicial review.
Monarchy	• Drawn close to political controversy through the attempted prorogation of Parliament in 2019. • Reported criticisms of the Rwanda deportation policy by then Prince of Wales, Charles, created the impression of tension between the monarchy and the government.[60]
Church of England	• Various bishops took critical stances towards the government over suspected lockdown violations by Dominic Cummings and later the Rwanda policy.[61]
British Broadcasting Corporation (BBC)	• Subject to political pressure, including from the Cabinet member within whose portfolio it fell, Nadine Dorries. As secretary of state for digital, culture, media, and sport, Dorries, who has a track record of being critical of the BBC (as well as of praising it),[62] on one occasion implied (prematurely) by a tweet that the licence fee was due to be abolished, calling into doubt the funding basis of the corporation.[63]

To obtain a fuller view of how the approach of the Johnson era could contaminate and undermine institutions, it is worth considering the position of one particular body: the Civil Service. This is another institution for which the Johnson period was one of wilfully orchestrated unease and disruption.[64] Despite the Civil Service being a part of the government, and being critical to its success, participants in the Johnson administration publicly seemingly called into question its worth, in the process breaking with the restraint that might normally be expected in this regard.[65] The Priti Patel case gave rise to concern about the behaviour of a senior minister towards officials, and was connected to the abrupt departure of a permanent secretary.[66]

In this general environment, it is worth considering the experience of the Civil Service during 2019–22 against its key statement of principles, the *Civil Service Code*, key excerpts of which are set out here:[67]

Civil Service values…
The Civil Service is an integral and key part of the government of the United Kingdom. It supports the government of the day in developing and implementing its policies, and in delivering public services. Civil servants are accountable to ministers, who in turn are accountable to Parliament…

Standards of behaviour

Integrity

You must:
- fulfil your duties and obligations responsibly
- always act in a way that is professional and that deserves and retains the confidence of all those with whom you have dealings

- carry out your fiduciary obligations responsibly (that is make sure public money and other resources are used properly and efficiently)
- deal with the public and their affairs fairly, efficiently, promptly, effectively and sensitively, to the best of your ability
- ensure you have Ministerial authorisation for any contact with the media
- keep accurate official records and handle information as openly as possible within the legal framework
- comply with the law and uphold the administration of justice

You must not:
- misuse your official position, for example by using information acquired in the course of your official duties to further your private interests or those of others
- accept gifts or hospitality or receive other benefits from anyone which might reasonably be seen to compromise your personal judgement or integrity
- disclose official information without authority (this duty continues to apply after you leave the Civil Service)

Honesty

You must:
- set out the facts and relevant issues truthfully, and correct any errors as soon as possible
- use resources only for the authorised public purposes for which they are provided

You must not:
- deceive or knowingly mislead ministers, Parliament or others
- be influenced by improper pressures from others or the prospect of personal gain

Objectivity

You must:
- provide information and advice, including advice to ministers, on the basis of the evidence, and accurately present the options and facts
- take decisions on the merits of the case
- take due account of expert and professional advice

You must not:
- ignore inconvenient facts or relevant considerations when providing advice or making decisions

- frustrate the implementation of policies once decisions are taken by declining to take, or abstaining from, action which flows from those decisions

Impartiality

You must:
- carry out your responsibilities in a way that is fair, just and equitable and reflects the Civil Service commitment to equality and diversity

You must not:
- act in a way that unjustifiably favours or discriminates against particular individuals or interests

Political Impartiality

You must:
- serve the government, whatever its political persuasion, to the best of your ability in a way which maintains political impartiality and is in line with the requirements of this code, no matter what your own political beliefs are
- act in a way which deserves and retains the confidence of ministers, while at the same time ensuring that you will be able to establish the

same relationship with those whom you may be required to serve in some future government
- comply with any restrictions that have been laid down on your political activities

You must not:
- act in a way that is determined by party political considerations, or use official resources for party political purposes
- allow your personal political views to determine any advice you give or your actions.

Rights and responsibilities

Your department or agency has a duty to make you aware of this Code and its values.

If you believe that you are being required to act in a way which conflicts with this Code, your department or agency must consider your concern, and make sure that you are not penalised for raising it.

If you have a concern, you should start by talking to your line manager or someone else in your line management chain. If for any reason you would find this difficult, you should raise the matter with your department's nominated officers who have been appointed to advise staff on the code.

If you become aware of actions by others which you believe conflict with this code you should report this to your line manager or someone else in your line management chain; alternatively you may wish to seek advice from your nominated officer. You should report evidence of criminal or unlawful activity to the police or other appropriate regulatory authorities. This code does not cover HR management issues.

If you have raised a matter in accordance with the relevant procedures, and do not receive what you consider to be a reasonable response, you may report the matter to the Civil Service Commission...

If the matter cannot be resolved using the procedures set out above, and you feel you cannot carry out the instructions you have been given, you will have to resign from the Civil Service.

This Code is part of the contractual relationship between you and your employer. It sets out the high standards of behaviour expected of you which follow from your position in public and national life as a civil servant. You can take pride in living up to these values.

A consideration of the fulfilment of these principles in the context of the Johnson administration should begin with a particular observation. Like many aspects of the UK constitution, they rest to a significant extent on commitment to them not only from officials but also from ministers. In the absence of such a quality on the part of the latter, its possession by the former – though essential – is insufficient. As the code sets out, civil servants answer to the political heads of government, and officials have a limited range of options when confronted by improper or troubling conduct or policy decisions. We have already identified numerous areas of concern involving the political leadership of the UK government. Between them, they have negative implications across all four standards identified in the *Civil Service Code*.

Let's start with 'Integrity'. The revelations of lockdown parties, including the police findings and those of the Sue Gray report, reveal many shortcomings. Responsibility, professionalism, and compliance with the law were all lacking. Furthermore, the prohibition on acceptance of 'gifts or hospitality ... from anyone' if doing so could 'be seen to compromise your personal judgement or integrity' was contravened in a way that the drafters of this text surely could not have foreseen. On 15 May 2020, officials were brought wine and cheese by the prime minister from his Downing Street flat for consumption at a gathering (comprising 'a number of separate meetings') in the Number 10 garden, of which a photograph was taken.[68] The police decided that this particular event did not meet 'the threshold for criminal investigation'.[69] But the episode does not reflect well on the prime minister (who is also, we should note, minister for the Civil Service) in fulfilling his responsibility to avoid undermining standards. Further failings from the 'Integrity' perspective include handling of official records, which surfaced in the context of inquiries into the funding of the Downing Street flat renovation, and the complaints Lord (Christopher) Geidt made when serving as independent adviser on ministers' interests.[70] The House of Commons Committee of Public Accounts – as noted on p. 18 – complained of 'poor record-keeping' in its inquiry into the award of pandemic-related contracts.[71]

The maintenance of integrity, the code notes, means that officials should not 'disclose official information without authority'. It adds that 'this duty continues to apply after you leave the Civil Service'. In July 2022, when the government offered misleading accounts of the context for the Pincher case, a former permanent secretary felt obliged to intervene publicly to correct them, drawing on his first-hand knowledge.[72] This episode illustrates how failures to adhere to constitutional standards can force others to respond in ways that seem to violate further norms. It should also be noted that this part of the code applies to special advisers (who are exempt from the 'Objectivity' and 'Impartiality' requirements but subject to 'Integrity' and 'Honesty'). The conduct of Dominic Cummings since his acrimonious exit from Number 10 late in 2020 is also difficult to reconcile with the stipulation that civil servants, even those who have left their posts, need to maintain confidentiality around 'official information'.[73]

Next, 'Honesty'. In May 2020, an anonymous employee posted a complaint on the official Civil Service

Twitter account – soon removed – about working for 'truth twisters'.[74] Perhaps this covert act was indicative of broader discontent among civil servants about the misleading presentation of information associated with the Johnson administration. If ministers are determined to take a manipulative approach in this regard, it is difficult for officials to resist them. They might become directly embroiled in less than candid messaging through such means as drafting and issuing press releases that make dubious use of statistics, or the misleading briefing of journalists. The lockdown events are once again relevant here. The Gray report produced evidence of officials approaching these gatherings in a furtive manner, seeking to conceal them from the outside world. Gray, for instance, cited a message sent from a special adviser to the prime minister's principal private secretary in May 2020 reading:

> Drinks this eve is a lovely idea so I've shared with the E & V team who are in the office. Just to flag that the press conference will probably be finishing around that time, so helpful if people can be mindful of that as speakers and cameras are leaving, not walking around waving bottles of wine etc.[75]

Third, 'Objectivity'. It seems likely that, during the Johnson premiership, the Whitehall environment was less conducive than it might have been to the provision of honest advice from civil servants to ministers. Events such as the abrupt departure of multiple senior officials, for instance, are not suggestive of an atmosphere hospitable to the raising of difficult issues. There have also been signs of the government pressing ahead with policies – potentially of a constitutionally controversial nature – without giving due consideration to factors such as evidence or expert opinion.[76] The requirement to implement decisions once taken without resistance forces officials ultimately to comply with such practices, unless willing to take more drastic – even career-ending – action. A future inquiry into the pandemic response might reveal further significant evidence in this area.

The frequency of turnover in high-level Whitehall officials in the Johnson era also has implications for the fourth standard, 'Impartiality'. If a minister or prime minister is seen to be connected to the displacement of one civil servant and their replacement by another, there is a chance that the latter – however honest their intentions – will be perceived as personally aligned to the politician in question. A threat is thereby posed to 'Political Impartiality' as defined in the code. Future ministers and prime ministers might have doubts about the suitability of officials who came to their posts in this way, and perhaps will contemplate making their own appointments, thereby reinforcing the tendency further. This point has not yet clearly been reached, but it is conceivable that it could be. The 'Political Impartiality' portion of the *Civil Service Code* would at this point have lost viability. Even if an outcome this extreme does not transpire, there is potential for increased friction and distrust in intra-executive relationships.

The various issues discussed here lead us on to the question of how an official can raise concerns. A chief problem is that, once again, the various procedures set out were probably not designed to accommodate the possibility that people at the very highest level would be implicated in wrongdoing. The Gray report identified faults of this type with regards to the very centre of government. It noted, however, that steps had been taken to rectify the weaknesses.[77] A further response from Johnson to the findings of Gray was to announce an organisational overhaul at Downing Street. Following the appearance of her interim report, Johnson stated on 31 January 2022 that, to ensure that the 'leadership structures of Downing Street' met 'the demands of the expansion of Number 10', he was 'creating an Office of the Prime Minister, with a Permanent Secretary to lead Number 10'. Whether an administrative reconfiguration of this type was the primary answer to the problems of the Johnson era is debatable.[78] Certainly, whatever changes were pursued in this regard did not prevent the re-occurrence of difficulties, such as the Chris Pincher episode.

Johnson also recognised in his 31 January statement that 'it is time not just to review the Civil Service and Special Adviser codes of conduct wherever necessary …

but also to make sure those codes are properly enforced'.[79] That the Johnson governments were ever likely to attach substantial importance to such goals was always doubtful. The main framework for Civil Service policy at the time came from the 'Declaration on Government Reform', first published in June 2021. While making some reference to the subject, the declaration did not emphasise the importance of maintaining constitutional standards. Furthermore, while its core aims – enhancements across the fields of 'people', 'performance', and 'partnership'[80] – were not objectionable in themselves, there was certainly scope for concern about potential tensions between them (depending on how, precisely, they were implemented) and Civil Service values. They could, for instance, increase ministerial discretion with regards to appointments, and make the opinions of individuals a factor in their recruitment. Both tendencies could be problematic from the point of view of Whitehall principles such as objectivity and impartiality.[81]

Part Three

Recommendations and Conclusion

Recommendations

As Johnson moved on to the next stage in his career, he left behind him much work for those committed to a functioning democratic UK constitution. If it is possible to extract any positives from the Johnson experience, they will be achieved by treating it as a stress test. Johnson has revealed, augmented, and created weaknesses in the UK political system. These vulnerabilities will persist after his departure. Taking into account the necessity for action in the post-Johnson era, in this chapter we discuss means of addressing the problems exposed by the foregoing assessment of the Johnson premiership. To reiterate, these areas of concern include:

- Poor conduct that does not necessarily violate any specific rule;
- The violation of rules without clear legal basis such as conventions;

- Unlawful activities of a constitutionally challenging nature;
- Violations of criminal law by ministers;
- Willingness to break with treaty obligations and international law; and
- The compromising of public institutions and the values associated with them.

We can add a further item to this list of constitutionally objectionable traits. Not only was the Johnson administration prone to departing from and undermining norms but it also displayed a tendency to evade, belittle, or erode any mechanisms that might serve to limit it (such as Parliament, the courts, and other oversight bodies), particularly in its efforts to perpetrate constitutional violations of the type discussed in this work. As we noted in the first part of this book, in as far as self-regulation fails to operate, we are dependent on such structures. The Johnson governments both ignored important voluntary restraints, and also set out to undermine other limitations. Moreover, such enhancements as they did introduce to the regulatory system were limited. In May 2022, for instance, responding to recommendations from the CSPL, Johnson gave the independent adviser on ministers' interests the ability to initiate investigations of possible breaches of the *Ministerial Code* (previously the adviser could only carry out such an inquiry if asked to by the premier). But, rather than making the exercise of this authority fully autonomous, as CSPL recommended, he made it contingent upon the approval of the prime minister. Some other important aspects of the CSPL agenda (see Appendix 3) were rejected outright.[1]

These tendencies demonstrate that existing means of constitutional regulation in the UK need enhancement. Any proposals advanced need to take into account that they are directed towards a system that allowed Johnson and his allies both to ascend and frisk within it. He attained the highest office in UK politics and occupied it for three years despite a proclivity for malpractice that was widely known long before 2019, and which he confirmed repeatedly as prime minister. Eventually, the system self-corrected. What the late Professor George Jones described as the elasticity of the premiership manifested itself. The restraints were stretched, surely far further than is normal, but eventually they snapped back, all the harder for the extent to which they had been tested. Yet, by this point, much damage had been permitted, both of a short term and likely more lasting nature. Furthermore, it would be a mistake to assume that impulses of the type associated with the Johnson administration will vanish forever with him. Any changes, therefore, must be directed towards addressing weaknesses that allowed these developments and episodes to occur; towards the additional problems added under Johnson; and towards more difficulties that might come.

The underlying challenges faced are considerable, and greater than those aroused by any one individual, however objectionable their conduct might be. To succeed, future remedies need to seek to address the whole of the problem, rather than simply parcelling up aspects of it. With this observation in mind, it is important to examine the essential aspects of a constitution. They involve both patterns of behaviour, and the framework within which such activity takes place. For although accounts of constitutional systems sometimes distinguish between culture and structures,[2] it is important not to treat them as though they are mutually exclusive entities. In fact they are part of a whole.

Rules and institutions are the product of an environment: it shapes them and they in turn influence it. Any effort to strengthen and improve a constitution must allow for this interrelationship. It should certainly be central to attempts to deal with the apparent failure of individuals to moderate their own conduct and subordinate their own perceived interests to a wider whole. No democratic constitution can function satisfactorily without the presence within it of individuals of good intention and sound judgement. Their absence is principally a problem of culture. But it may be possible to develop mechanisms that encourage and facilitate such good practice, and which provide safety mechanisms on those occasions when it fails to materialise.

With this concern in mind, in what follows, we set out proposals intended to protect more effectively the key features of the UK constitution, as set out in documents including the *Seven Principles of Public Life*, *The Cabinet Manual*, and the *Ministerial Code*. Our main purpose, then, rather than altering values themselves, is to propose new ways of realising and enforcing them. In many cases, the aim is to create structures that could help avoid objectionable developments before they take place, as well as identifying and seeking to correct them after they have occurred. In this sense, they might not need to be used actively at all, or at least only rarely. They would, if successful, help create a desire to adhere to rules, combined with a perception that to transgress would carry with it costs that outweighed possible advantages.

We group our recommendations into three broad categories: relatively straightforward and already on the agenda; more ambitious; and of the most extensive type. To support action under one heading does not preclude adoption of ideas in another; indeed they could be complementary. But the grouping gives an idea of the amount of time and commitment likely to be involved, and how great the implied potential change. Most of them would require, among other preconditions, the firm and sustained support of a UK government and prime minister. An immediate or later successor to Johnson may wish to make a firm break with his constitutional approach. They might seek to rectify the damage incurred during his premiership and prevent similar occurrences in future. If of such an inclination, they might find some of the options on offer, from the relatively modest to the ambitious, below.

Immediate steps

The problem we face is twofold: an apparent willingness of senior figures to depart from constitutional norms has in turn revealed frailties in the protections against such conduct. Strengthening those protections can help address both these problems and their combined effect. It might encourage greater awareness of and respect for the rules, and also provide for their harder enforcement. Various relevant proposals are already on the agenda. They include the proposals made in August 2021 by the Nigel Boardman inquiry into the use of supply chain finance in government, which focus on the promotion of integrity in particular with respect to interactions between ministers, officials, and outside financial interests.[3] A special concentration on how to strengthen judicial independence is found in the measures advocated by the All-Party Parliamentary Group on Democracy and the Constitution in its June 2022 publication.[4] The Constitution Unit of University College London issued in July 2022 a set of proposals intended to strengthen five regulatory bodies with remits of a constitutional nature.[5] Of particular significance for present purposes (though they met with a less than enthusiastic response from the

Johnson government) are the thirty-four recommendations that emerged from the CSPL 'Standards Matter' project, the final output of which appeared in November 2021 (reproduced in Appendix 3).[6] This programme includes within it measures intended to enhance ethical regimes within Whitehall applying to ministers and civil servants, through such means as the clarification and strengthening of rules, new procedures, creating rights and obligations, greater transparency, and providing the commissioner for public appointments, the Advisory Committee on Business Appointments, and the independent adviser on ministers' interests with more autonomy and a statutory basis.

The independent adviser on ministers' interests focuses on a text the contents of which are central to our book: the *Ministerial Code*. The 'Standards Matter' project has also taken a close interest in this document. Among the various stipulations intended to make the *Ministerial Code* more effective and independently enforced, the 'Standards Matter' report states that it 'should be reconstituted solely as a code of conduct on ethical standards' (Recommendation 3). CSPL takes the view that, to avoid confusion that is detrimental to the effectiveness of the text, the provisions presently contained in the code that deal with 'political and constitutional principles' and 'processes of Cabinet government' should be removed and included in *The Cabinet Manual*, in which some of the relevant material is already placed.[7] Subject to our previously advanced proviso that constitutional and ethical standards, while they can in some senses be distinguished, are closely connected or even overlapping, we see this proposal as presenting an important opportunity.

The government has confirmed that it is in the process of redrafting *The Cabinet Manual*. This initiative is welcome. The previous edition is an invaluable official statement by the UK executive of the position from its perspective across a range of areas of the UK constitution. But it is now more than a decade old. Changes that have occurred since 2011 – such as the UK's exit from the EU and the repeal of the Fixed-term Parliaments Act 2011 – need to be reflected in the manual. A useful principle to adopt would be that of updating the document at the start of each new Parliament. This approach would make it possible to avoid anachronism, while avoiding more continuous change that might create confusion and encourage the impression of an unstable text. As well as updating content, a new edition of the manual could help clarify and strengthen constitutional values in key areas. It could do so partly by restating provisions already contained in the existing text but with which the Johnson governments have had difficulty complying, such as the requirement that ministers adhere to the law, including international law and treaty commitments. The manual could also prescribe new guidance to ministers to ensure they behave in a way that is supportive of wider constitutional values, for instance:

- Principles that prime ministers should adhere to when requesting a dissolution of Parliament from the monarch, to ensure that the ability to trigger a general election is not abused;
- Clarification of circumstances in which it is and is not appropriate to seek a prorogation of Parliament;
- Guidance on 'caretaker' principles that should apply to an outgoing prime minister who remains in office while their successor is determined;
- Clarification of how the government should respond to efforts by the Opposition to table no-confidence motions, including matters involving their precise wording;
- How to avoid behaviour that compromises the ability of officials to adhere to the *Civil Service Code*;
- Means of adherence to the Sewel convention, which stipulates that the UK Parliament will not normally legislate for devolved matters without the agreement of devolved legislatures; and proper forms of consultation and joint decision-making with the devolved institutions;
- Stipulations regarding appropriate ways to respond to legal decisions and how to protect the judiciary from attacks on its integrity, including from within the executive, and the ways in which all ministers should promote the rule of law;

- Details of the basis on which scrutiny of the conferral of peerages and honours is received and acted upon;
- Detailed guidance on what does and does not constitute an appropriate degree of openness on the part of ministers in dealing with Parliament, and what amounts to the misleading of it, knowingly or otherwise; and
- Principles to apply to the creation and use of delegated law-making powers.

In including such content, the authors of the manual would need expressly to recognise what is already an implicit reality: that – despite currently protesting to the contrary – the text is more than simply a reflection of the constitutional position. Through describing arrangements, it forms a part of them, influencing perception and thereby helping to determine what they are.[8] Given the importance of a document with such a function, the process by which the next edition is produced should be as transparent and inclusive as possible, with wide public consultation at UK and devolved level.

A further potential development involving the status of documents such as *The Cabinet Manual* and the *Ministerial Code* is presently in its tentative stages, though it may come about more fully in future. The courts have begun to show an interest in treating them (in particular the *Ministerial Code*) as justiciable, specifically through a judgment issued by the High Court in December 2021. In a discussion of this subject, it stated:

> We accept that the Ministerial Code has no statutory basis but that of itself is not conclusive. We accept that the interpretation of parts, perhaps most, of the provisions of the Ministerial Code would not be justiciable because they involve political matters (such as references to collective Cabinet responsibility) or ministerial relations with Parliament. Such matters are intended to be subject to the judgement of the Prime Minister not the courts. But it does not follow that all parts of the Ministerial Code should be treated as non-justiciable.[9]

Perhaps in future, then, the judiciary will take the provisions of codes into account when reviewing the actions of ministers for their compliance with the law or otherwise. It is difficult to speculate about the possible future development of case law. We could expect the courts to approach the use of these texts cautiously. They would not seek directly to impose all of their contents and would surely sidestep consideration of decisions about matters such as the retention or removal from office of ministers. Perhaps a potential application of this justiciability could be in circumstances in which a former civil servant felt that their continued employment had been made untenable by ministerial actions that in some way transgressed key principles set out in a code. In this sense, constitutional principles could receive indirect enforcement from the courts – a significant development.[10]

Further reform

The above approach is perhaps best described as breathing new life into nostrums of the past – the carriers of the checks and balances that together bring equipoise to the British constitution. Our analysis suggests that the UK constitution faces challenges that Johnson has helped expose but that are greater than any one individual (even – with all his manifest defects – Johnson himself). This observation in turn suggests that, while immediate measures are required, more extensive attention to the problem is also necessary. With this need in mind, we make recommendations for changes that do not yet have the same degree of currency as those discussed in the section above, but that we believe merit consideration. We begin with the office of prime minister. Government – as we have stressed – is about more than the person who holds this post, the functions they perform, and the team that supports them. But premiers are vital in providing a lead and promoting adherence to constitutional standards. We therefore propose the introduction of an oath of office for UK prime ministers.

Lord Howarth of Newport raised this idea during an

oral evidence session of the House of Lords Select Committee on the Constitution, of which he is a member, in March 2022. He put it to Richard Heaton, the former permanent secretary at the Ministry of Justice, and Sir Jonathan Jones, the former Treasury Solicitor (both of whom were receptive to the suggestion) that:

> If we think it is a good thing that the Lord Chancellor takes this solemn and hallowed oath of office, which anchors that individual in the role and helps to define what it is, and at the same time affirms certain constitutional principles, would you see benefit in other Ministers, including the Prime Minister, taking an equally solemn oath that expands their role beyond the privy councillor's oath and equally helps define what it is that constitutes their duty in office?[11]

At a subsequent session of the Select Committee on the Constitution in July 2022, Dominic Grieve expressed the opinion that:

> sometimes symbolism, including oath-taking, is the usual way we do it in this country, and we could require someone who now has a very well-established constitutional position, even though it has emerged in an undefined way, namely the Prime Minister, to make a public statement on taking office of a kind that involves the taking of an oath in front of an

appropriate audience, which would probably be Parliament. One cannot think where else it would be. If that has a reinforcement of standards, it may serve a useful purpose, and I do not think we should, therefore, ignore the possibility that it could be beneficial.[12]

We find these arguments persuasive. Introducing this practice for prime ministers could emphasise their own commitment to the principles contained in the key constitutional codes, and to ensuring that others adhered to them. This measure would be, as Grieve suggested, of symbolic importance, assisting public understanding of and expectations regarding the conduct of government. It would also enhance the status of the rules concerned within government and those responsible for enforcing them. A premier who had made such a commitment might find it harder to evade responsibility for misconduct. Prime ministers could swear the oath publicly in the Chamber of the House of Commons, in the presence of the speaker, when first taking on the premiership, and perhaps if continuing in office after a general election. We propose the following text:

THE PRIME MINISTER'S OATH

To uphold the principle and practices of collective Cabinet government.

To uphold and respect the conventions and expectations contained in THE MINISTERIAL CODE, THE CABINET MANUAL, and THE SEVEN NOLAN PRINCIPLES OF PUBLIC LIFE.

To sustain the impartiality of the Civil and Diplomatic Services, the Intelligence and Security Services, and the Armed Forces.

and to have constant regard for THE CIVIL SERVICE CODE and THE SPECIAL ADVISERS' CODE.

To account personally to Parliament and its select committees for all the above.

To uphold the rule of law in all circumstances.

One of the most constitutionally problematic aspects of the Johnson administration was the nature of its relationship with Parliament. It resisted accountability to the legislature in various ways, and sought to deploy its law-making power for dubious purposes. To prevent such abuses from occurring in future, and to promote constitutional compliance, Parliament – given its status as the supreme institution within the system of representative democracy – should take on a more assertive role in defining and enforcing standards, in particular those that apply to the executive.

There is no obvious reason why the prime minister should possess principal responsibility for drafting and interpreting a number of the rules contained within the *Ministerial Code*, and Parliament might in some cases seem more suited for the task – for instance, in determining whether it has been misled, knowingly or otherwise, and if so what the consequence should be. Only in the most extreme circumstances did it prove possible for the House of Commons even to instigate an inquiry into the actions of Johnson by its Privileges Committee. Aside from the question of how this particular initiative will work out in practice, it is significant that the task of investigating possible abuses by the prime minister has been entrusted to a committee, rather than being left solely to a debate and vote in the full House. Such bodies are far more likely to achieve the consensus needed for meaningful action over constitutional matters. It is for this reason that we advocate measures centring on committees.

The system of select committees in the House of Commons was introduced in its current form in 1979. These bodies have grown over time both in the scope of their work and their degree of independence from party whips and the executive. There are various ways in which these committees might be harnessed to help tackle contemporary problems with the UK constitution. Potentially, their role in overseeing public appointments might be extended – at least in some cases – to enable them formally to veto ministerial choices, as a means of averting the potential abuse of patronage. We note various discussions have taken place over time about codifying 'contempts' and privileges and placing them on a statutory basis.[13] If implemented they might strengthen the ability of select committees to secure the evidence they have judged as needed in the course of their work. Providing Commons select committees with a more established role in the legislative process could enable them to challenge any problems, including those of a constitutional nature, with bills and perhaps statutory instruments.

Another means of deploying the specialist focus of these bodies would be to help with the problem of dubious statements by ministers in the House. It might be useful to establish a mechanism whereby members could refer claims in a given policy area to the relevant select committee, to provide an assessment of their veracity or otherwise. The committee might then be able to refer matters back to the House, which could – if appropriate – require action from the minister concerned, such as the correction of any inaccuracy. Sufficient resources would need to be made available to support this function. Some cases of alleged misleading of Parliament could fall outside of this procedure. For instance, the various answers Johnson gave when asked about gatherings during times of Covid restrictions did not involve claims about matters such as statistics within a specific policy area. A means of dealing with issues of this nature that does not require full authorisation from the plenary on individual occasions would require more substantial change.

If Parliament is to take fuller responsibility for upholding constitutional standards on its own account, then structural and procedural innovation is required. We propose the establishment of a Joint Committee on Constitutional Standards, without a majority for any one party, perhaps chaired by a former justice of the Supreme Court, lord chief justice (of England and Wales, or of Northern Ireland) or lord president of the Court of Session (of Scotland), drawn from the House of Lords cross benches. Working closely with relevant specialist committees in both Houses, this body could produce regular reports on the general operation of the system of constitutional standards and compliance, including the various codes and mechanisms for their promotion. It could, when necessary, investigate individual cases of alleged misconduct or problematic policy initiatives. When required, it could make recommendations to Parliament for action. Furthermore, the committee could produce draft statements of those constitutional principles for which Parliament as a whole wished to take responsibility, which it deemed too important to be left to the executive alone to describe and uphold. In so doing, it could consolidate various constitutional principles and rules that are at present distributed across different locations into a single document. Such a text could be submitted to the two Houses for approval and thereafter incorporated into the work of the Joint Committee.

A further task for the Joint Committee would be to consider whether more extensive change was required. It should give consideration to the possibility of establishing a full-time office, akin to the comptroller and auditor general, for the oversight of constitutional standards, to support the work of the committee. A wider potential constitutional change to assist the functioning of such a system would involve an alteration in the working practices of the executive. This measure would be the introduction to the Civil Service of an equivalent to the accounting officer principle, but for constitutional issues. It would apply if a secretary of state or other minister had decided to adopt a course of action that gave rise to defined constitutional concerns. It might involve, for instance, a legislative or policy initiative that seemed incompatible with the international rule of law; personal conduct that was inappropriate or involved conflicts of interest; or the misleading presentation of information. An official asked to facilitate such action could raise it with their permanent secretary or equivalent, who could require a direction to proceed, which – if the political leadership insisted on continuing – would be lodged with the Joint Committee. We do not anticipate that this safeguard would need to be used frequently. But its existence could act as an important protective barrier for officials, and would discourage ministers from embarking upon improper behaviour and policies.

A new framework

The recommendations proposed so far represent adjustments and augmentations broadly within the existing constitutional framework of the UK. It might be that more extensive insurance is needed, that the frailties the Johnson governments have – through their bonfire of the decencies – revealed, created, and perhaps foreshadowed, are so severe that we must go further in establishing protective mechanisms. What if, for instance, the abuses perpetrated under Johnson are a prelude to something worse? Though he channelled certain ideas and forces that might be seen as undermining the democratic system, Johnson seemed motivated less by ideological concerns and more by personal ambitions and weaknesses, with the constitution suffering collateral damage. But might another leader at some point in the future, perhaps observing the openings discovered by Johnson, seek to exploit them for more overtly malign general objectives, as opposed to personal satisfaction?

In the light of recent experience, entirely to exclude such a possibility might seem complacent. Even if – as we profoundly hope – it does not come about, it is sensible to consider whether more can and should be done to uphold constitutional standards against greater and lesser threats. The final possibility we suggest here is intended, like the others, both to strengthen formal protections and promote a culture of adherence. It would, we hope, encourage and provide guidance to those who wish to adhere to the rules, and dissuade and create barriers to those who do not.

There is an ongoing debate in the UK about whether or not it would be desirable to adopt a 'written' or 'codified' constitution.[14] The idea does not belong specifically to any one part of the political spectrum, and it has had both supporters and opponents spread across it. Much of the UK constitution is of course written down – in places such as Acts of Parliament, parliamentary regulations, judicial decisions, and the various codes discussed in this book. A 'written' or 'codified' constitution would set out what its authors believed to be the most important components of the political system in a single text. It would deal with matters such as the role of institutions and the relationship between them, and the rights of members of the public.

To appreciate the significance of such a document, rather than considering the full list of contents it might contain, it is useful to recognise the core function it would perform. It would identify principles and rules that are of a higher level of importance than others and take precedence over them. This status would be realised by two central means. The first would be through enforcement of the constitution, to ensure that actions by public authorities or laws – including even Acts of Parliament – that conflicted with the constitution were legally void. The task of upholding the constitution in this way would probably be entrusted to the judiciary, with the Supreme Court the ultimate arbiter. The second way in which the special status of the constitution would be secured is through an amendment procedure. Any changes to the text would require a higher level of consensus than alterations to more normal laws. They might, for instance, involve the attainment of some kind of parliamentary supermajority, or agreement at devolved level, or approval via referendum.

Without such mechanisms in place, it would be possible for Parliament to override the constitution in the same way it can supplant any other laws, and therefore the text would not achieve the protections that might be hoped of it. Here is the central reason why a 'written' or 'codified' constitution would represent such a highly significant shift in the nature of the UK legal-political order. It would entail a decisive movement away from a doctrine often held to be central to the UK constitution, known as parliamentary sovereignty or supremacy. According to this principle, Parliament is legally unlimited in its power to make and unmake any law, and cannot be constrained by any higher authority. In as far as this concept is intellectually coherent, it is incompatible with the existence of a constitutional text, protected by a special amendment procedure and subject to enforcement by a court.

Here is not the place for a full account of the extensive debate about the desirability or otherwise of establishing a 'written' or 'codified' constitution. But for present purposes it is worth considering one of the main arguments often given against such an initiative: that there is no pressing need for such a demanding and potentially divisive project.[15] It is therefore relevant to ask: how far have recent developments increased the need for this change, and have they done so decisively?

A first factor is the impact of departure from the EU. While the UK was a member, it was required to conform to European law, including the Charter of Fundamental Rights, which in this sense performed functions similar to those associated with a 'written' or 'codified' constitution. Exit from the EU has removed this constraint upon the actions of a UK government working through Parliament, and as yet no controlling mechanism has been provided in its place. Indeed the prospect of removing limitations formed part of the case made for Brexit by its exponents. A 'written' or 'codified' constitution could replace the stabilising and restraining apparatus that has been lost.[16]

Second is the specific constitutional abuses perpetrated by the Johnson governments. We should not claim that such a text would necessarily and directly have prevented all of them. But it could provide safeguards firmer than

THE BONFIRE OF THE DECENCIES

those previously available in important areas. It might include provisions to protect the autonomy of institutions and office holders with constitutional oversight roles, such as the independent adviser on ministers' interests, the Civil Service Commission, and the Electoral Commission. It might also entrench protections for human rights, such as the right to protest and the rights of refugees, and make stipulations about when it is appropriate to recommend prorogations and dissolutions of Parliament. A 'written' or 'codified' constitution could specify the powers of the judiciary, reducing the potential for ministers to seek to denigrate or circumscribe the courts. It might contain measures to ensure approval was secured from the devolved legislatures before the UK Parliament could pass laws that impacted upon their spheres of operation.

The establishment of a text of this type is not a task to undertake lightly, but it should be given full consideration by those who believe the Johnson experience has revealed serious weaknesses that need correction. In giving evidence to the House of Lords Select Committee on the Constitution in June 2022, Lord (Kenneth) Clarke, drawing on many years of experience at the highest level as a Conservative politician, provided an illustration of how opinion might shift in this direction. As part of a discussion of the possible failure of self-regulation, he asked:

Can we any longer rely on an unwritten constitution, its conventions and the assumption that the entire political class will feel themselves bound by them? In the past, I have always respected my opponents on that front, on the basis that I may disagree with their policies, but the underlying conventions of politics and the standards in public life are as strongly accepted by my political opponents as by my political friends. You can no longer be so sure of that.[17]

For those who conclude that a 'written' constitution is a necessity, vital to the success of such a project would be the extent to which it could claim democratic legitimacy, and that the contents of the text commanded consensus (though universal agreement would never be possible). Various mechanisms could ensure cross-party engagement at UK level, as well as a devolved input, and possibly the incorporation of members of the public (see box on p. 143). A collectively owned document would possess greater force and provide a basis on which politicians and public alike might better understand and adhere to the constitution of the UK. It might include a preamble that defined succinctly the principle of a self-regulating institutional order, using updated terminology, for which the text that followed would be a rule book and, where necessary, legal support mechanism. One aspect of the system – that of parliamentary sovereignty – would have been discarded to protect others.

To engage the public in the process of establishing a 'written' or 'codified' constitution, one or more of the following models could be employed.

Model	Comment
'Great and good' exercise	A Royal Commission or similar body composed of prominent figures could hold public hearings and seek contributions from both more specialist and general sources. It could be a preparatory stage leading on to a more inclusive exercise.
Elected body	Either a specially elected assembly or one made up of existing elected representatives, possibly from different tiers of governance (e.g. the House of Commons, devolved legislatures, and local authorities). Both it and the citizens' convention described below could deliberate and make decisions about the content of a constitutional text to be taken forward for ratification.
Citizens' convention	A body made up of members of the public, probably chosen through a random selection process ('sortition'). There is now substantial precedent for such an initiative, internationally and from within the UK.
Ratification	The text might be approved either by elected representatives, perhaps with a supermajority requirement of some kind, or through a referendum.

Conclusion: Poetry, Plumbing, and Purpose

The condition, vitality, and robustness of the British constitution has become a first-order question inside the political society it has a duty to protect. In the past, traditional approaches – written and human – brought a strange charm and genuine flexibility to the task of repairing and reinvigorating the constitution, both in its poetry as well as its plumbing, its declaratory principles as well as the mechanics of their operation. But muddling through is no longer enough. The experience of the Johnson premiership demonstrated a fragility at the very heart of our unsystematic system, for the prime protector of the norms and procedures that animate the decencies and probity of public and political life turned out to be a wrong 'un, who repeatedly resisted the application of those very requirements to himself. In 10 Downing Street, for three whole years, they were not known at this address.

However, Mr Johnson's legacy to his country could be the stimulation of a serious look at its constitutional procedures, the associated paperwork, and the patterns of behaviour needed to keep the United Kingdom safely in the very highest ranks of the rule-of-law nations – a gift until recently so securely banked that we did not have to worry about it.

Yet anxiety can be our spur. A new settlement our aim. Fatalism laced with mute acceptance our foe. We must banish pessimism and replace it with a spirit of mutual cooperation and shared, practical purpose if the 2020s are not to succumb to the rancour, recrimination, and incivility that has scarred the twenty-first century so far. It is a moment for refreshment and reform. They are ours for the taking.

APPENDICES

Appendix 1

Timeline of Constitutionally Significant Events

1951: UK ratifies European Convention on
Human Rights.

1954: Crichel Down affair sees Thomas Dugdale MP
resign as minister for agriculture and fisheries, in
what was perceived as a recognition in classic form of
the principle of individual ministerial responsibility.

1954: UK ratifies 1951 United Nations Refugee
Convention.

1956: Suez Crisis involving collusion between UK,
France, and Israel to regain control of nationalised
Suez Canal.

1963: John Profumo MP resigns as secretary of state for
war for having misled Parliament.

1963: Transition from Harold Macmillan to Alec Douglas-Home as prime minister generates controversy about the use of the royal prerogative, bringing the monarchy closer to political controversy than it has tended to be in the democratic era.

1966: UK introduces right of individuals to petition the European Court of Human Rights to access their rights under the European Convention on Human Rights.

1973: UK accedes to the European Communities.

1979: System of House of Commons select committees, monitoring the work of specific Whitehall departments, is introduced, building on earlier experiments from the 1960s onwards.

1992: *Questions of Procedure for Ministers*, a document traceable as far back as the 1940s, and with precursors dating to 1917, is published for the first time. From 1997 it appeared under the title of *Ministerial Code*. It has never had a statutory basis.

1995: Committee on Standards in Public Life issues *The Seven Principles of Public Life*.

1996: *Civil Service Code* first issued, without a statutory basis.

1998: Human Rights Act incorporates European Convention on Human Rights into UK domestic law.

Belfast/Good Friday Agreement reached, forming the key component of the Northern Ireland Peace Process. Approved by referendums in both Northern Ireland and the Republic of Ireland.

1999: Devolved institutions begin operating in Wales, Scotland, and Northern Ireland.

2000: Political Parties, Elections and Referendums Act provides a regulatory framework for elections and referendums, and a statutory basis for the Electoral Commission.

2003: Controversial invasion of Iraq led by United States, with UK one of the participating countries.

2005: Constitutional Reform Act establishes UK Supreme Court (which begins operating from 2009), reforms the office of lord chancellor, and creates Judicial Appointments Commission.

2010: 'Wright reforms' to the House of Commons select committee system, with members elected by party caucuses and chairs elected by the whole House, reducing the influence of the whips.

Constitutional Reform and Governance Act provides Civil Service, and *Civil Service Code*, with a statutory basis.

2011: *The Cabinet Manual* is published.

Fixed-term Parliaments Act passed.

2016: Referendum on continued European Union membership produces a 'leave' result.

2018: Amber Rudd MP resigns as home secretary for inadvertently misleading Parliament.

2019: Boris Johnson becomes prime minister and Conservatives win general election later in the same year.

2020: UK exits the European Union.

2022: Johnson agrees, on 7 July, to a Conservative leadership contest to determine his replacement.

Queen Elizabeth II dies on 8 September; the Prince of Wales becomes King Charles III.

United Kingdom Constitution Monitoring Group Statement of Principles

NB. This text provides an example of how it is possible to construct, largely from existing official sources, a comprehensive set of written constitutional principles against which the performance of the UK government and other public institutions can be judged.

Nature of UK constitution, and constitutional change

1. It is essential that the constitutional arrangements of the UK are clear and knowable; that they should be, wherever possible, subject to robust and impartial enforcement; and that they should as far as possible command consensus. Constitutional change should take place in a considered fashion and as far as possible on a basis of consensus. The legislative authority of the UK Parliament should be exercised subject to underlying

constitutional principles including those outlined in this text.

Representative democracy

2. The UK is a representative democracy. The existence of devolved and UK governments is derived from the broad support of the respective legislatures (see e.g.: *Cabinet Manual*, 2011, paragraph 2). The UK House of Commons and the devolved legislatures in turn derive legitimacy from the free and fair election of their members held at intervals of no more (except in the most exceptional of circumstances) than four or five years.

Governments and their accountability to legislatures

3. Ministers are accountable, individually or collectively, to their legislatures for the exercise of their ministerial responsibilities, and for the activities of the publicly funded bodies within their remits (see e.g.: *Ministerial Code*, 2019, paragraph 1.3b). Ministers must provide information that is both accurate and truthful to their respective legislatures, and should correct unintended errors they make as soon as possible (see e.g.: *Ministerial Code*, paragraph 1.3c). Devolved and UK ministers should be as open as they can in their interactions with legislatures and the public. They

should withhold information only if to do otherwise would compromise the public interest, as set out in freedom of information legislation and other specific legislation (see e.g.: *Ministerial Code*, paragraph 1.3d).

4. Governments should not use their powers to compromise the ability of legislatures autonomously to perform the constitutional functions they carry out on behalf of the public, such as holding the executive to account and making law.

5. At UK level, the House of Commons is rightly acknowledged as in a position of primacy over the House of Lords. But the House of Lords has a legitimate role in parliamentary processes, including scrutiny of primary and delegated legislation, and its special interest and expertise in constitutional matters should be acknowledged.

6. 'Civil servants are accountable to ministers, who in turn are accountable to Parliament' (*Civil Service Code*, 2015). There are limited exceptions to this general principle, including the role of specific officials (Accounting Officers or, in Scotland, Accountable Officers), who at UK level are personally responsible to the House of Commons Committee of Public Accounts 'for keeping proper accounts; for the avoidance of waste and extravagance; and for the efficient and effective use of resources' (*Ministerial Code*, paragraph 5.3). Similar

THE BONFIRE OF THE DECENCIES

exceptions apply at devolved level, with officials accountable for financial management to devolved legislatures.

Legal powers and obligations of ministers

7. 'Ministers are under an overarching duty to comply
with the law, including international law and treaty obligations, uphold the administration of justice, and protect
the integrity of public life. They are expected to observe
the Seven Principles of Public Life: selflessness, integrity,
objectivity, accountability, openness, honesty, and leadership' (*Cabinet Manual,* paragraph 3.46...).

8. UK and devolved ministers' powers are derived from
legislation; ministers may also exercise powers derived
from the common law, including prerogative powers of
the Crown. Ministerial powers should normally be speci-
fied in primary rather than secondary legislation. Such
powers are subject to limits and constraints; they should
be exercised, and public expenditure approved, only for
the purposes authorised by the relevant legislation, and
in accordance with established norms and reasonable
expectation. The exercise of ministerial powers should
only exceptionally be immune from challenge in the
courts (see e.g.: *Cabinet Manual,* paragraph 3.24).

9. [UK] 'ministers must ensure that no conflict arises,

or could reasonably be perceived to arise, between their public duties and their private interests, financial or otherwise' (*Ministerial Code*, paragraph 7.1). 'Ministers must not use government resources for Party political purposes' (*Ministerial Code*, paragraph 1.3i). These principles extend to devolved ministers also, and all holders of public office.

Civil Service

10. Civil servants, with the exceptions of 'special advisers' and certain others, must be 'recruited on merit on the basis of fair and open competition'. They should be promoted on merit usually following a competitive process. They must be required to 'carry out their duties with integrity and honesty, and objectivity and impartiality'. They must serve the government to the best of their ability in a way that maintains political impartiality, and act in a way that deserves and retains the confidence of ministers in the government of the day, while ensuring they will be able to establish the same relationship with those they may be required to serve in a future government (see: *Constitutional Reform and Governance Act 2010*, Part 1 for the UK, Scottish, and Welsh governments; *Civil Service Codes;* and similar provisions for the Northern Ireland Civil Service).

11. [UK] 'ministers must uphold the political impartiality of the Civil Service, and not ask civil servants to act in any way which would conflict with the Civil Service Code and the requirements of the Constitutional Reform and Governance Act 2010' (*Ministerial Code*, paragraph 5.1j). [UK] 'ministers have a duty to give fair consideration and due weight to informed and impartial advice from civil servants, as well as to other considerations and advice in reaching policy decisions, and should have regard to the Principles of Scientific Advice to Government' (*Ministerial Code*, paragraph 5.2). These principles extend to devolved ministers also.

12. 'Special advisers' to ministers are temporary civil servants who are not required to be recruited on merit through competition or to carry out their duties with objectivity and impartiality. They are an accepted part of government but should act in accordance with prescribed limitations (see: *Constitutional Reform and Governance Act 2010*, Part 1: *Special Advisers Codes, and similar provisions in Northern Ireland*).

Devolution and the Union

13. The devolved institutions of Wales and Scotland are 'permanent' parts of the United Kingdom constitution (see: *Scotland Act 2016*, section 1; *Wales Act 2017*, section 1).

The devolved institutions of Northern Ireland are also constitutional fixtures; subject to the proviso that Northern Ireland can, after approval via a referendum, leave the UK (once the UK Parliament has legislated to this effect) and join the Republic of Ireland. The UK government has previously conceded the principle that Scotland could become independent from the UK subject to a referendum.

14. In those spheres of operation that have been devolved in Wales, Scotland, and Northern Ireland, or those devolved in Scotland and Northern Ireland but not in Wales, responsibility for those functions in relation to England or England and Wales are exercised by 'UK government' ministers answerable to the UK Parliament.

15. The devolved institutions have the right to legislative and executive autonomy in their respective spheres of operation. 'The UK Government will proceed in accordance with the convention that the UK Parliament would not normally legislate with regard to devolved matters except with the agreement of the devolved legislature' (*Memorandum of Understanding*, 2013, paragraph 14; see also: *Scotland Act 2016*, section 2; *Wales Act 2017*, section 2). The devolved institutions have a proper interest in decisions taken at UK level that impact upon them, and over international agreements entered into by the UK when their implementation would fall within devolved competence.

16. Appropriate structures, regulations, and practices should exist to ensure that the principles set out in items 13 and 15 above are fully realised. They should allow in particular for liaison, coordination, and genuine co-decision-making between devolved and UK executives; and between devolved and UK legislatures.

The judiciary and the rule of law

17. 'The judiciary interprets and applies the law; and develops the common law in its decisions. It is a long-established constitutional principle that the judiciary is independent of both the government of the day and Parliament so as to ensure the even-handed administration of justice. Civil servants, ministers and, in particular, the Lord Chancellor are under a duty to uphold the continued independence of the judiciary, and must not seek to influence particular judicial decisions' (*Cabinet Manual*, paragraph 16; see also: *Justice (Northern Ireland) Act 2002*, section 1; *Constitutional Reform Act 2005*, part 2; *Judiciary and Courts (Scotland) Act 2008*).

18. 'The courts scrutinise the manner in which ministers' powers are exercised. The main route is through the mechanism of judicial review, which enables the actions of a minister to be challenged on the basis that [they] did not have the power to act in such a way (including

on human rights grounds); that the action was unreasonable; or that the power was exercised in a procedurally unfair way' (*Cabinet Manual*, paragraph 3.39). 'The devolution statutes impose additional constraints on the competence of devolved ministers.'

19. The activities described in 17 and 18 must be recognised as central to the maintenance of the rule of law. All institutions and office holders dealt with in these principles are required to promote the rule of law. It encompasses concepts including the law being clear and possible to know; access to the law; equality before the law; governors and governed alike being subject to the law; impartiality in the application of the law; adherence to international law; and the protection of human rights.

Constitutional monarchy

20. The monarchy should not be drawn into party political controversy. The powers formally attached to the monarchy should not be deployed in ways that undermine the principles outlined in this text.

Appendix 3

Recommendations from the Committee on Standards in Public Life[1]

Recommendation 1

The Civil Service should review its approach to enforcing ethical standards across government, with a view to creating a more rigorous and consistent compliance system, in line with the recommendation of the Boardman report.

Recommendation 2

The government should pass primary legislation to place the independent adviser on ministers' interests, the public appointments commissioner, and the Advisory Committee on Business Appointments [ACOBA] on a statutory basis.

Recommendation 3

The *Ministerial Code* should be reconstituted solely as a code of conduct on ethical standards.

Recommendation 4

A requirement for the prime minister to issue the *Ministerial Code* should be enshrined in primary legislation.

Recommendation 5

The independent adviser should be consulted in any process of revision to the *Ministerial Code*.

Recommendation 6

The *Ministerial Code* should detail a range of sanctions the prime minister may issue, including, but not limited to, apologies, fines, and asking for a minister's resignation.

Recommendation 7

The independent adviser should be appointed through an enhanced version of the current process for significant public appointments.

Recommendation 8

The independent adviser should be able to initiate investigations into breaches of the *Ministerial Code*.

Recommendation 9

The independent adviser should have the authority to determine breaches of the *Ministerial Code*.

Recommendation 10

The independent adviser's findings should be published no more than eight weeks after a report has been submitted to the prime minister.

Recommendation 11

The business appointment rules should be amended to prohibit for two years appointments where the applicant has had significant and direct responsibility for policy, regulation, or the awarding of contracts relevant to the hiring company.

Recommendation 12

The business appointment rules should be amended to allow ACOBA and government departments to issue a ban on lobbying of up to five years.

Recommendation 13

The lobbying ban should include a ban on any work for lobbying firms within the set time limit.

Recommendation 14

The government should make adherence to the business appointment rules an enforceable legal requirement for ministers, civil servants, and special advisers, and set out what the consequences for a breach of contract may be.

Recommendation 15

ACOBA rulings should be directly binding on applicants.

Recommendation 16

ACOBA should have the power to undertake investigations into potential breaches of the business appointment rules, and be granted additional resources as necessary. The Cabinet Office should decide on sanctions or remedial action in the case of a breach.

Recommendation 17

Government departments should publish anonymised and aggregated data on how many applications under the business appointment rules are submitted, approved, or rejected each year.

Recommendation 18

The Cabinet Office should ensure the business appointment rules are applied consistently across all government departments, and work with ACOBA to promote best practice and awareness of the rules.

Recommendation 19

The Governance Code for Public Appointments should be amended to make clear that ministers should not appoint a candidate who is deemed unappointable by an assessment panel, but if they do so, the minister must appear in front of the relevant select committee to justify their decision.

Recommendation 20

The Governance Code should be amended so that ministers must consult with the commissioner for public appointments on the composition of all panel members for competitions for significant appointments.

Recommendation 21

Senior independent panel members should have a specific duty to report to the commissioner on the conduct of significant competitions.

Recommendation 22

The chairs of ACOBA and HOLAC [House of Lords Appointment Commission], the registrar of consultant lobbyists, the commissioner for public appointments, and the independent adviser on ministers' interests should all be appointed through the process for significant public appointments, and the assessment panel for each should have a majority of independent members.

Recommendation 23

Chairs of standards committees should chair assessment panels for the appointment of their independent members.

Recommendation 24

Government departments should publish a list of all unregulated and regulated public appointments.

Recommendation 25

The appointments process for non-executive directors of government departments should be regulated under the Governance Code for Public Appointments.

Recommendation 26

The Cabinet Office should collate all departmental transparency releases and publish them in an accessible, centrally managed, and searchable database.

Recommendation 27

The Cabinet Office should provide stricter guidelines on minimum standards for the descriptions of meetings and ensure compliance by government departments.

Recommendation 28

The government should publish transparency returns monthly, rather than quarterly, in line with the MPs' and peers' registers of interests.

Recommendation 29

The government should include meetings held between external organisations, directors general, and directors in transparency releases.

Recommendation 30
The government should include meetings held between external organisations and special advisers in transparency releases.

Recommendation 31
The government should update guidance to make clear that informal lobbying, and lobbying via alternative forms of communication such as WhatsApp or Zoom, should be reported to officials.

Recommendation 32
The government should revise the categories of published information to close the loophole by which informal lobbying is not disclosed in departmental releases.

Recommendation 33
Consultant lobbyists should also have to register on the basis of any communications with special advisers, directors general, and directors.

Recommendation 34
Consultant lobbyists should have to declare the date, recipient, and subject matter of their lobbying.

Appendix 4

A note on literature and methods

This work has a polemical dimension. But it also engages with, and adds to, concepts found in secondary literature in the fields of politics and contemporary history. It adds to the literature on prime ministers in a variety of ways. It is an early contribution to what will inevitably become a substantial body of work, from various authors and perspectives, considering the full term of the Boris Johnson administration. Our particular perspective is the constitutional impact and implications of his governments. We expect others will consider this particular theme, since it is arguably the most prominent feature of the Johnson premiership and is at least one of the most central. This work also adds to the extensive and longstanding debate about the role and power of the office of prime minister, to which we have both contributed previously, along with numerous others.[2] We also add – through a specific focus on the constitution in the Johnson era – to the more general debate about the UK executive and its internal and external power dynamics.[3]

Beyond this particular focus, we approach, from the point of view of our subject matter, the ongoing development of the UK constitution – the existing literature on which has not yet fully taken on, but will benefit from, an assessment of the Johnson era.[4] We are also able to take forward the existing discussion of the implications of Brexit for the UK political system.[5] Finally, we consider the UK constitution under Johnson from the point of view of debate about the idea of international democratic backsliding and the rise of forces such as populism.[6] Some of this literature suggests that the UK has followed these tendencies.[7] This work enables us to explore this possibility more fully, using its specific focus.

Our principal tasks for the main body of the work are to analyse the constitutional approach taken during the Johnson premiership; to place it in wider context; to assess its implications; and to measure performance against constitutional norms. We draw upon various primary sources including memoirs and diaries; official reports of various kinds; and media coverage. To establish a set of criteria against which events and tendencies during 2019–22 can be judged, we draw on a variety of official statements of principle, some of which have developed over a number of decades, and to which the UK executive (and other institutions) are supposedly committed.[8]

Notes

Epigraph

1. Spoken during a brief visit the Queen was paying to a seminar at Queen Mary University of London (at which one of us was present) discussing the document *Questions of Procedures for Ministers* (later titled *Ministerial Code*), which had recently been declassified and published by then prime minister John Major.

2. 'His Majesty the King's address to the nation and Commonwealth', royal.uk (10 September 2022), available at: <https://www.royal.uk/his-majesty-king%E2%80%99s-address-nation-and-commonwealth>, last accessed 10 September 2022.

3. Frances Gibb, 'Lord Mackay: "Margaret Thatcher stuck to the rules. Boris Johnson didn't"', *Times Magazine* (30 July 2022).

4. 'His Majesty The King's Declaration', royal.uk (10 September 2022), available at: <https://www.royal.

uk/his-majesty-kings-declaration>, last accessed 10 September 2022.

5. 'His Majesty The King's reply to addresses of condolence at Westminster Hall', royal.uk (12 September 2022), available at: <https://www.royal.uk/his-majesty-kings-reply-addresses-condolence-westminster-hall>, last accessed 12 September 2022.

Introduction

1. House of Lords Select Committee on the Constitution, *Respect and Co-operation: Building a Stronger Union for the 21st Century*, HL Paper 142 (20 January 2022), p. 15.

2. Lord Judge, 'Constitutional Change: Unfinished Business'. Lecture delivered at University College London (4 December 2013).

3. W. E. Gladstone, *Gleanings of Past Years, vol 1* (London: John Murray, 1879), p. 245.

4. Priestley referred to the 'good chaps theory of government' at an Adam Smith Institute conference at St George's Windsor in 1985, speaking to a group of officials from the Ronald Reagan administration. See: Clive Priestley, 'Promoting the efficiency of central government' in Arthur Shenfield et al., *Managing the*

Bureaucracy (London: Adam Smith Institute, 1986), p. 117; Peter Hennessy, '"Harvesting the Cupboards": Why Britain has Produced no Administrative Theory or Ideology in the Twentieth Century', *Transactions of the Royal Historical Society*, 4 (1994), p. 205.

Part One: The Nature of the Problem

1. 'Boris Johnson "forgot" about Chris Pincher groping claims', *ITV News* (2022), available at: <https://www.itv.com/news/2022–07–05/pm-briefing-in-person-about-complaint-against-pincher-before-whip-appointment>, last accessed 15 July 2022.

2. Tamara Cohen, 'Former civil servant bulldozes through No 10's defence of disgraced MP Chris Pincher', *Sky News* (5 July 2022), available at: <https://news.sky.com/story/civil-servant-bulldozes-through-no-10s-defence-of-disgraced-mp-chris-pincher-12646138>, last accessed 15 July 2022.

3. Rowena Mason, 'New chancellor Zahawi tells Johnson to go as Donelan quits after 48 hours in job', *Guardian* (7 July 2022), available at: <https://www.theguardian.com/politics/2022/jul/07/new-chancellor-zahawi-tells-johnson-to-go-as-

donelan-quits-after-48-hours-in-job>, last accessed 14 July 2022.

4. George Parker, Sebastian Payne, and Jim Pickard, 'Power seeps away from Boris Johnson', *Financial Times* (6 July 2022), available at: <https://www. ft.com/content/657efa45–7fbe-4b8e-bd64-e32d57a9c7bb>, last accessed 15 July 2022.

5. Ben Quinn, 'Top Tories resist moves to speed up replacing Boris Johnson as party leader', *Guardian* (8 July 2022), available at: <https:// www.theguardian.com/politics/2022/jul/08/ top-tories-resist-moves-to-speed-up-replacing-boris-johnson-as-party-leader>, last accessed 14 July 2022.

6. 'No 10 blocks Labour "no confidence" vote on government and Boris Johnson', *BBC News* (12 July 2022), available at: <https://www.bbc.co.uk/ news/uk-politics-62139269>, last accessed 14 July 2022.

7. Email from Eleanor Updale to Peter Hennessy (18 September 2022).

8. William Hague, 'Tories must beware Boris the incredible sulk', *The Times* (25 July 2022), available at <https://www.thetimes.co.uk/article/tories-must-beware-boris-the-incredible-sulk-m5lsbmjtb>, last accessed 25 July 2022.

9. For analysis of the ministerial revolt against Johnson and the motives for it, see: Laura

Kuenssberg, 'Boris Johnson: The inside story of the prime minister's downfall', *BBC News* (13 July 2022), available at: <https://www.bbc.co.uk/news/uk-politics-62150409>, last accessed 16 July 2022.

10. Cabinet Office, *The Cabinet Manual: A Guide to the Laws, Conventions and Rules on the Operation of Government*, 1st Edition (London: Cabinet Office, 2011), pp. 2–3, available at: <https://assets.publishing.service.gov.uk/government/uploads/system/uploads/attachment_data/file/60641/cabinet-manual.pdf>, last accessed 25 May 2022.

11. One of the present authors is editor of the UKCMG bi-annual reports.

12. Committee on Standards in Public Life, *Upholding Standards in Public Life: Final Report of the Standards Matter 2 Review* (London: Committee on Standards in Public Life, 2021), available at: <https://assets.publishing.service.gov.uk/government/uploads/system/uploads/attachment_data/file/1029944/Upholding_Standards_in_Public_Life_-_Web_Accessible.pdf>, last accessed 2 July 2022. For an expression of this view, see p. 53.

13. *Ministerial Code* (London: Cabinet Office, 2022), p. 1, available at: <https://assets.publishing.service.gov.uk/government/uploads/system/uploads/attachment_data/file/1079310/Ministerial_Code.pdf>, last accessed 12 June 2022.

14. *Civil Service Code* (London: 2015), available at: <https://www.gov.uk/government/publications/civil-service-code/the-civil-service-code>, last accessed 19 June 2022.

15. For the principles that apply in this regard, see: *Ministerial Code*, pp. 2, 16–19.

16. See e.g.: *Civil Service Code*.

17. This point is made by Jesse Norman in his letter withdrawing support from Boris Johnson as leader of the Conservative Party: 'Letter to the Prime Minister', *Jesse Norman* website, available at: <https://www.jessenorman.com>, last accessed 30 July 2022.

18. David Parsley and Jane Merrick, 'Home Office civil servants challenged "callous" Rwanda migrant policy' (15 April 2022), available at: <https://inews.co.uk/news/home-office-civil-servants-challenged-callous-rwanda-migrant-policy-1579449>, last accessed 14 July 2022.

19. Diane Taylor, Rajeev Syal, and Emine Sinmaz, 'Rwanda asylum flight cancelled after 11th-hour intervention ECHR intervention', *Guardian* (14 June 2022), available at: <https://www.theguardian.com/uk-news/2022/jun/14/european-court-humam-right-makes-11th-hour-intervention-in-rwanda-asylum-seeker-plan>, last accessed 25 August 2022.

20. For exploitation of the UK approach to the

Northern Ireland Protocol by the Chinese government, see Chinese Embassy in Ireland (@ChinaEmbIreland), '"2 years ago we made a promise to the Northern Ireland Protocol. We are determined to break it."', Twitter (1 July 2022), available at: <https://twitter.com/ChinaEmbIreland/status/1542908356448354304?ref_src=twsrc%5Etfw>, last accessed 24 September 2022.

21. 'Covid-19 Inquiry Terms of Reference' (28 June 2022), available at: <https://covid19.public-inquiry.uk/wp-content/uploads/2022/06/Covid-19-Inquiry-Terms-of-Reference-Final.pdf>, last accessed 14 July 2022.

22. See e.g.: Annette Dittert, 'The politics of lies: Boris Johnson and the erosion of the rule of law', *New Statesman* (15 July 2021), available at: <https://www.newstatesman.com/politics/2021/07/politics-lies-boris-johnson-and-erosion-rule-law>, last accessed 4 May 2022. For a complaint about smears from a former Conservative MP and minister, see: Jon Stone, 'Boris Johnson is an "integrity vacuum" who turned No.10 into a "cronyistic cabal" says former Tory legal chief', *Independent* (24 April 2021), available at: <https://www.independent.co.uk/news/uk/politics/boris-johnson-cronyism-integrity-vacuum-cabal-

dominic-grieve-b1836853.html>, last accessed
4 May 2022.

23. See e.g.: Richard Cockett, *Twilight of Truth:
Chamberlain, Appeasement and the Manipulation of
the Press* (London: Weidenfeld & Nicolson, 1989).

24. Lucy Atkinson, Andrew Blick, and Matt
Qvortrup, *The Referendum in Britain: A History*
(Oxford: Oxford University Press, 2020),
pp. 69–70.

25. For Johnson on this episode see: Boris Johnson,
The Churchill Factor: How One Man Made History
(London: Hodder & Stoughton, 2014), p. 124.

26. See: Peter Hennessy, *The Prime Minister: The
Office and its Holders Since 1945* (London: Allen
Lane, 2000), pp. 217–47. For a historic perspective
on Johnson, including an Eden comparison, see
e.g.: Philip Stephens, 'Boris Johnson's lies are
plunging Britain into a dark morass', *Financial
Times* (19 September 2019), available at: <https://
www.ft.com/content/645d8786-d9f2-11e9-8f9b-
77216ebe1f17>, last accessed 25 May 2022.

27. Nick Duffy, 'Nadine Dorries and Jacob Rees-
Mogg lead loyalists rallying round PM despite
"minor mistake" over Chris Pincher', *I* (5 July
2022), available at: <https://inews.co.uk/news/
politics/nadine-dorries-jacob-rees-mogg-lead-
loyalists-rallying-round-pm-despite-minor-

mistake-chris-pincher-1725489>, last accessed 14 July 2022.

28. For an overview see e.g.: Andrew Blick (ed.), *The Constitution in Review: Second Report from the United Kingdom Constitution Monitoring Group* (London: Constitution Society, 2022), available at: <https://consoc.org.uk/wp-content/uploads/2022/02/UK-Constitution-Monitoring-Group-Second-Report.pdf>, last accessed 25 May 2022.

29. See e.g.: Chris Patten, 'Boris Johnson and the Virtue of Accountability', *Project Syndicate* (10 December 2021), available at: <https://www.project-syndicate.org/commentary/boris-johnson-christmas-parties-government-accountability-by-chris-patten-2021–12>, last accessed 4 May 2022.

30. See e.g.: an interview Jacob Rees-Mogg gave to Julia Hartley-Brewer for *Talk Radio* on 13 April 2022 regarding the fixed penalty notice served on Johnson and its implications. Available at: <https://www.youtube.com/watch?v=GrmdCxP5TYk>, last accessed 7 May 2022.

31. See e.g.: 'Fourth senior civil servant announces exit in six months', *BBC News* (9 July 2020), available at: <https://www.bbc.co.uk/news/uk-politics-53351672>, last accessed 5 May 2022.

32. Rowena Mason and Aubrey Allegretti, 'Boris Johnson defies calls to quit after he and Rishi Sunak fined', *Guardian* (12 April 2022), available at: <https://www.theguardian.com/politics/2022/apr/12/boris-johnson-and-rishi-sunak-fined-for-breaking-covid-lockdown-laws>, last accessed 5 July 2022.

33. Andrew Blick, 'Removing a Prime Minister', *The Constitution Society Blog* (28 April 2022), available at: <https://consoc.org.uk/removing-a-prime-minister/>, last accessed 31 July 2022.

34. Kieran Devine, Daniel Dunford, and Ganesh Rao, 'Boris Johnson suffers more ministerial resignations than any PM in modern history', *Sky News* (7 July 2022), available at: <https://news.sky.com/story/boris-johnson-suffers-more-resignations-in-one-day-than-any-prime-minister-in-history-12647012>, last accessed 31 July 2022.

35. Samuel Lovett, 'Sajid Javid resignation letter in full as "team player" health secretary quits: "You have lost my confidence"', *Independent* (6 July 2022), available at: <https://www.independent.co.uk/news/uk/politics/savid-javid-resignation-letter-boris-johnson-b2116400.html>, last accessed 31 July 2022.

36. Emily Atkinson, 'Rishi Sunak's damning resignation letter to Boris Johnson in full', *Independent* (5 July 2022), available at: <https://

www.independent.co.uk/news/uk/politics/rishi-sunak-resignation-letter-boris-johnson-b2116416.html>, last accessed 31 July 2022.

37. Hague, 'Tories must beware Boris the incredible sulk'.

38. Jesse Norman, 'Letter to the Prime Minister'.

39. Hennessy, *The Prime Minister: The Office and its Holders Since 1945*, p. 468.

40. Committee on Standards in Public Life, *The Seven Principles of Public Life* (London: Committee on Standards in Public Life, 1995), available at: <https://www.gov.uk/government/publications/the-7-principles-of-public-life/the-7-principles-of-public-life--2>, last accessed 24 September 2022.

41. Andrew Sparrow, '"Operation Save Big Dog": who is in the line of fire at No 10?', *Guardian* (16 January 2022), available at: <https://www.theguardian.com/politics/2022/jan/16/operation-save-big-dog-who-is-in-line-of-fire-no-10-boris-johnson-partygate>, last accessed 10 June 2022.

42. Jesse Norman, 'Letter to the Prime Minister'.

43. *Findings of the Second Permanent Secretary's Investigation into Alleged Gatherings on Government Premises During Covid Restrictions* (London: Cabinet Office, 2022), pp. 12–13, available at: <https://assets.publishing.service.gov.uk/government/

uploads/system/uploads/attachment_data/
file/1078404/2022–05–25_FINAL_FINDINGS_
OF_SECOND_PERMANENT_SECRETARY_
INTO_ALLEGED_GATHERINGS.pdf>, last
accessed 10 June 2022.

44. Heather Stewart, Peter Walker, and Jessica Elgot,
'Delegation of cabinet ministers heads to No 10
to demand Johnson quit', *Guardian* (6 July 2022),
available at: <https://www.theguardian.com/
politics/2022/jul/06/michael-gove-boris-johnson-
more-ministers-resign>, last accessed 16 July 2022.

45. For discussion of the calculations involved, see:
Pippa Catterall, 'To oust or not to oust? Why
Johnson has faced a much easier ride from Tory
MPs than Margaret Thatcher', *LSE British Politics
and Policy* (28 April 2022), available at: <https://
blogs.lse.ac.uk/politicsandpolicy/to-oust-or-not-
to-oust-johnson/>, last accessed 16 July 2022.

46. See e.g.: Independent Adviser on Ministers'
Interests, *Annual Report* (May 2021), paras 20–34,
available at: <https://assets.publishing.service.
gov.uk/government/uploads/system/uploads/
attachment_data/file/990394/Report_by_the_
Independent_Adviser_May_2021__1_.pdf>, last
accessed 10 June 2022.

47. See e.g.: Aubrey Allegretti and Heather Stewart,
'Boris Johnson backs attempt to protect Owen
Paterson from sleaze watchdog', *Guardian*

(3 November 2021), available at: <https://
www.theguardian.com/politics/2021/nov/03/
appalling-double-standards-labour-criticises-tory-
attempts-to-save-owen-paterson>, last accessed 10
June 2022.

48. 'Covid: Government's PPE "VIP lane" unlawful,
court rules', *BBC News* (12 January 2022), available
at: <https://www.bbc.co.uk/news/uk-59968037>,
last accessed 14 July 2022.

49. House of Commons Committee of Public
Accounts, *Government's Contracts with Randox
Laboratories Ltd*, Seventeenth Report of
Session 2022–3, HC 28 (London: House of
Commons, 2022), p.3, available at: <https://
committees.parliament.uk/publications/23257/
documents/169721/default/>, last accessed 31
July 2022.

50. Andrew Blick (ed.), *The Constitution in Review:
First Report from the United Kingdom Constitution
Monitoring Group* (London: Constitution Society,
2022), p. 40, available at: <https://consoc.org.
uk/wp-content/uploads/2021/09/UKCMG-
CONSTITUTION-IN-REVIEW-1.pdf>, last
accessed 17 July 2022.

51. Jessica Elgot, 'Liz Truss halts Dominic Raab's bill
of rights plan', *Guardian* (7 September 2022),
available at: <https://www.theguardian.com/law/

2022/sep/o7/liz-truss-halts-dominic-raab-bill-of-rights-plan>, last accessed 16 September 2022.

52. Blick, *The Constitution in Review* 2, p. 41.

53. See e.g.: Aubrey Allegretti, 'Tory whips accused of threatening rebels with loss of local funding', *Guardian* (15 September 2021), available at: <https://www.theguardian.com/politics/2021/sep/15/tory-whips-accused-threatening-rebels-loss-local-funding>, last accessed 10 June 2022.

54. On the lack of evidence the policy would have the 'deterrent effect' claimed for it, see: Ione Wells, 'Patel warned of uncertainty over Rwanda plan's deterrent effect', *BBC News* (17 April 2022), available at: <https://www.bbc.co.uk/news/uk-politics-61133983>, last accessed 14 July 2022.

55. Conservative Party, *Get Brexit Done, Unleash Britain's Potential: The Conservative and Unionist Party Manifesto 2019* (London: Conservative Party, 2019), p. 3, available at: <https://assets-global.website-files.com/5da42e2cae7ebd3f8bde353c/5dda924905da587992a064ba_Conservative%202019%20Manifesto.pdf>, last accessed 27 May 2022.

56. Fintan O'Toole, 'Boris Johnson's "oven ready" Brexit had a secret footnote: we'll rehash it later', *Guardian* (10 September 2020), available at: <https://www.theguardian.com/commentisfree/2020/sep/10/boris-johnson-oven-ready-brexit-cummings-withdrawal-agreement>,

last accessed 27 August 2022. For the UK government position, see: Liz Truss, 'The Northern Ireland Protocol must be changed to protect the hard-won peace here' (20 January 2022), available at: <https://www.gov.uk/government/speeches/the-northern-ireland-protocol-must-be-changed-to-protect-the-hard-won-peace-here-article-by-liz-truss>, last accessed 11 June 2022.

57. Fintan O'Toole, 'Britain's attack on its own protocol is one more exercise in Brexit gaslighting', *Guardian* (15 June 2022), available at: <https://www.theguardian.com/commentisfree/2022/jun/15/britain-ni-protocol-brexit-ministers-deal>, last accessed 16 July 2022.

58. Lord Evans, 'The government should go beyond a "low level of ambition" on the Ministerial Code', *Committee on Standards in Public Life Blog* (1 June 2022), available at: <https://cspl.blog.gov.uk/2022/06/01/the-government-should-go-beyond-a-low-level-of-ambition-on-the-ministerial-code/>, last accessed 11 June 2022.

59. For the changing tone of executive criticism of the judiciary, see e.g.: All-Party Parliamentary Group on Democracy and the Constitution, *An Independent Judiciary: Challenges Since 2016* (London: Institute for Constitutional and Democratic Research, 2022), pp. 32–7;

available at: <https://static1.squarespace.
com/static/6033d6547502c200670fd98c/t/6
2a05b38f1b9b809f61853ef/1654676281940/
SOPI+Report+FINAL.pdf>, last accessed 12
June 2022.

60. Aubrey Allegretti, 'Supreme Court judges
could be vetted by MPs in wake of prorogation
ruling', *Sky News* (30 September 2019),
available at: <https://news.sky.com/story/
supreme-court-judges-could-be-vetted-by-mps-
in-wake-of-prorogation-ruling-11822463>, last
accessed 31 July 2022.

61. All-Party Parliamentary Group on Democracy
and the Constitution, *An Independent Judiciary:
Challenges Since 2016*, p. 22.

62. Ibid., p. 23.

63. Ibid.

64. Dan Sabbagh, Luke Harding, and Andrew Roth,
'Russia report reveals UK government failed to
investigate Kremlin interference', *Guardian* (21
July 2020), available at: <https://www.theguardian.
com/world/2020/jul/21/russia-report-reveals-
uk-government-failed-to-address-kremlin-
interference-scottish-referendum-brexit>, last
accessed 16 July 2022.

65. David Conn, 'Matt Hancock acted unlawfully
by failing to publish Covid contracts', *Guardian*
(19 February 2021), available at: <https://

www.theguardian.com/society/2021/feb/19/
matt-hancock-acted-unlawfully-failing-publish-
covid-contracts-high-court>, last accessed 14
July 2022.

66. House of Commons Committee of Public
Accounts, *Government's Contracts with Randox
Laboratories Ltd*, p. 3.

67. Jim Pickard, 'Ministers resist Labour calls to
release Lebedev security advice', *Financial
Times* (12 May 2022), available at: <https://
www.ft.com/content/e891ed9c-d426–429f-8eab-
4db48c636ba2>, last accessed 10 June 2022.

68. See e.g.: Lisa O'Carroll, 'Dominic Cummings
says UK always intended to ditch NI protocol',
Guardian (13 October 2021), available at: <https://
www.theguardian.com/politics/2021/oct/13/
dominic-cummings-says-uk-always-intended-to-
ditch-ni-protocol-brexit>, last accessed 11 June
2022; Lisa O'Carroll, 'Boris Johnson promised to
tear up NI protocol, says DUP MP Ian Paisley',
Guardian (14 October 2021), available at: <https://
www.theguardian.com/politics/2021/oct/14/
boris-johnson-promised-to-tear-up-ni-protocol-
says-dup-mp-ian-paisley>, last accessed 28
August 2022.

69. Abbas Panjwani, 'Boris Johnson makes false
employment claim for ninth time in Parliament',
Full Fact (21 April 2022), available at: <https://

fullfact.org/economy/boris-johnson-makes-false-employment-claim-for-ninth-time-in-parliament/>, last accessed 10 June 2022.

70. Diane Taylor and Rajeev Syal, 'Home Office misled refugees about UN involvement in Rwanda plans, court told', *Guardian* (10 June 2022), available at: <https://www.theguardian.com/uk-news/2022/jun/10/home-office-misled-refugees-about-un-involvement-in-rwanda-plans-court-told>, last accessed 15 July 2022.

71. Kuenssberg, 'Boris Johnson: The inside story of the prime minister's downfall'.

72. Sophie Morris, 'Boris Johnson apologises for appointing Chris Pincher as deputy chief whip and said "it was the wrong thing to do"', *Sky News* (5 July 2022), available at: <https://news.sky.com/story/boris-johnson-apologises-for-appointing-chris-pincher-as-deputy-chief-whip-and-said-it-was-the-wrong-thing-to-do-12646408>, last accessed 30 July 2022.

73. 'Chris Pincher: Lord McDonald's letter in full', *BBC News* (5 July 2022), available at: <https://www.bbc.co.uk/news/uk-politics-62047757>, last accessed 30 July 2022.

74. Kuenssberg, 'Boris Johnson: The inside story of the prime minister's downfall'.

75. Cabinet Office, *Findings of the Second Permanent Secretary's Investigation into Alleged Gatherings*

on Government Premises During Covid Restrictions,
p. 36.

76. Cabinet Office, *The Cabinet Manual: A Guide to
the Laws, Conventions and Rules on the Operation of
Government,* pp. 2–3.

77. Lord True, minister of state, Cabinet Office,
to Baroness Drake, chair, House of Lords
Select Committee on the Constitution (7
February 2022), para 3, available at: <https://
committees.parliament.uk/publications/8813/
documents/89014/default/>, last accessed 15
July 2022.

78. Andrew Blick and Peter Hennessy, *The Hidden
Wiring Emerges: The Cabinet Manual and the
Working of the British Constitution* (London:
Institute for Public Policy Research, 2011), pp.
16–19, available at: <https://www.ippr.org/
files/images/media/files/publication/2011/08/
hiddenwiringemerges_Aug2011_7911.pdf>, last
accessed 15 July 2022.

79. The Supreme Court, R (on the application
of Miller) (Appellant) *v* The Prime Minister
(Respondent) Cherry and others (Respondents)
v Advocate General for Scotland (Appellant)
(Scotland), *On appeals from: [2019] EWHC 2381
(QB) and [2019] CSIH 49* (24 September 2019),
p. 3, available at: <https://www.supremecourt.uk/

cases/docs/uksc-2019-0192-summary.pdf>, last accessed 15 July 2022.

80. All-Party Parliamentary Group on Democracy and the Constitution, *An Independent Judiciary: Challenges Since 2016*, pp. 18–26.

81. Ibid., p. 55.

82. Blick, *The Constitution in Review 1*, pp. 23–4.

83. See e.g.: Alba Kapoor, 'Voter ID: a disproportionate solution to an invisible problem', *Runnymede Trust* blog (9 July 2021), available at: <https://www.runnymedetrust.org/blog/voter-id-a-disproportionate-solution-to-an-invisible-problem>, last accessed 16 July 2022.

84. Alex Dean, 'The Electoral Commission is now under government control. We should fear for UK democracy', *Prospect* (16 June 2022), available at: <https://www.prospectmagazine.co.uk/magazine/the-electoral-commission-is-now-under-government-control-fear-for-uk-democracy-john-pullinger-interview-elections-act>, last accessed 16 July 2022.

85. 'No 10 blocks Labour "no confidence" vote on government and Boris Johnson', *BBC News*.

86. 'Boris Johnson speaks to Queen after Supreme Court defeat', *Sky News* (24 September 2019), available at: <https://news.sky.com/story/boris-johnson-speaks-to-queen-after-supreme-court-ruling-11818771> last accessed 15 July 2022.

87. Allegretti, 'Supreme Court judges could be vetted by MPs in wake of prorogation ruling'.

88. See: 'PM "can't be trusted" on Brexit delay, Court of Session told', *BBC News* (4 October 2019), available at: <https://www.bbc.co.uk/news/uk-scotland-scotland-politics-49924755>, last accessed 31 July 2022. For the case in the Scottish Court of Session dealing with this matter, see: <https://www.scotcourts.gov.uk/docs/default-source/cos-general-docs/pdf-docs-for-opinions/2019csoh77.pdf?sfvrsn=0>, last accessed 31 July 2022.

89. For criticism of one law, the Elections Act 2022, both of its content and the way it was forced through Parliament, see: Toby James, 'Democracy undermined: elections in the UK are changing – here's how', *The Conversation*, available at: <https://theconversation.com/democracy-undermined-elections-in-the-uk-are-changing-heres-how-182251>, last accessed 16 July 2022.

90. 'Response from Sir David Norgrove to Alistair Carmichael MP – Use of official crime statistics by Prime Minister, Home Secretary and Home Office' (3 February 2022), available at: <https://uksa.statisticsauthority.gov.uk/correspondence/response-from-sir-david-norgrove-to-alistair-carmichael-mp-misuse-of-official-crime-statistics-

by-prime-minister-home-secretary-and-home-office/>, last accessed 19 June 2022.

91. Peter Foster, 'UK devolved governments attack Boris Johnson's post-Brexit plan', *Financial Times* (31 January 2022), available at: <https://www.ft.com/content/7dc8c707–71c6–4c85-ab3d-04464f5d16b9>, last accessed 16 July 2022.

92. Blick, *The Constitution in Review 2*, p. 37.

93. All-Party Parliamentary Group on Democracy and the Constitution, *An Independent Judiciary: Challenges Since 2016*, pp. 18–26.

94. E.g.: Suella Braverman, then attorney general. Heather Stewart, Rowena Mason, Jessica Elgot, and Peter Walker, 'Johnson clings on amid Cabinet standoff and dozens of resignations', *Guardian* (7 July 2022), available at: <https://www.theguardian.com/politics/2022/jul/06/johnson-clings-on-amid-cabinet-standoff-and-dozens-of-resignations>, last accessed 16 July 2022.

95. Becky Smith, 'DfE perm sec Jonathan Slater sacked over A-Level row', *Civil Service World* (26 August 2020), available at: <https://www.civilserviceworld.com/professions/article/dfe-perm-sec-jonathan-slater-sacked-over-a-level-row>, last accessed 16 July 2022.

96. Oliver Wright, 'Priti Patel inquiry: Boris Johnson condemned for refusing to throw cabinet bully overboard', *The Times* (21 November 2020),

available at: <https://www.thetimes.co.uk/article/
priti-patel-inquiry-boris-johnson-condemned-
for-refusing-to-throw-cabinet-bully-overboard-
cbzp9zjbb>, last accessed 16 July 2022.

97. Morris, 'Boris Johnson apologises for appointing
Chris Pincher as deputy chief whip and said "it
was the wrong thing to do"'.

98. Cabinet Office, *Findings of the Second Permanent
Secretary's Investigation into Alleged Gatherings
on Government Premises During Covid
Restrictions*, p. 36.

99. Rajeev Syal, 'The growing list of civil servants
frozen out while Johnson's ministers remain',
Guardian (26 August 2020), available at: <https://
www.theguardian.com/politics/2020/aug/26/
the-growing-list-of-civil-servants-frozen-out-
while-johnsons-ministers-remain>, last accessed 16
July 2022.

100. Cohen, 'Former civil servant bulldozes through
No 10's defence of disgraced MP Chris Pincher'.

101. 'Chris Pincher: Lord McDonald's letter in
full', *BBC News*.

102. All-Party Parliamentary Group on Democracy
and the Constitution, *An Independent Judiciary:
Challenges Since 2016*, pp. 17, 23, 24; Blick, *The
Constitution in Review 2*, p. 41.

103. All-Party Parliamentary Group on Democracy

and the Constitution, *An Independent Judiciary*, pp. 38–50.

104. 'UNHCR: UK asylum bill would break international law, damaging refugees and global co-operation', *UNHCR* (23 September 2021), available at: <https://www.unhcr.org/uk/news/press/2021/9/614c163f4/unhcr-uk-asylum-bill-would-break-international-law-damaging-refugees-and.html>, last accessed 16 July 2022.

105. O'Toole, 'Britain's attack on its own protocol is one more exercise in Brexit gaslighting'.

106. O'Carroll, 'Dominic Cummings says UK always intended to ditch NI protocol'; O'Carroll, 'Boris Johnson promised to tear up NI protocol, says DUP MP Ian Paisley'.

107. John Campbell, 'Brexit: EU says UK grace period extension breaches international law' (3 March 2021), *BBC News*, available at: <https://www.bbc.co.uk/news/uk-northern-ireland-56262527>, last accessed 16 July 2022.

108. Aubrey Allegretti, 'Northern Ireland protocol: what is the "doctrine of necessity"?', *Guardian* (13 June 2022), available at: <https://www.theguardian.com/politics/2022/jun/13/northern-ireland-protocol-what-is-the-doctrine-of-necessity>, last accessed 16 July 2022; Jonathan Jones, 'The Northern Ireland Protocol Bill: legal

(and perhaps illegal) goings on', *Institute for Government* (14 June 2022), available at: <https://www.instituteforgovernment.org.uk/blog/northern-ireland-protocol-bill>, last accessed 17 July 2022.

109. Mason and Allegretti, 'Boris Johnson defies calls to quit after he and Rishi Sunak fined'.

110. Richard Johnstone, '"Notwithstanding the breach of international law": government lawyers told internal market bill within civil service rules', *Civil Service World* (11 September 2020), available at: <https://www.civilserviceworld.com/professions/article/notwithstanding-the-breach-of-international-law-government-lawyers-told-cab-sec-says-internal-market-bill-within-civil-service-rules>, last accessed 16 July 2022.

111. Lizzie Dearden, 'Government officials told Priti Patel not to do asylum deal with Rwanda, court hears', *Independent* (19 July 2022), available at: <https://www.independent.co.uk/news/uk/home-news/rwanda-deal-priti-patel-asylum-law-b2126416.html>, last accessed 1 August 2022.

112. For views on the way in which Donald Trump through his behaviour tested the US Constitution during his 2017–21, presidency see e.g.: Ritu Prasa, 'US historians on what Donald Trump's legacy will be', *BBC News* (19 January 2021), available at: <https://www.bbc.co.uk/news/

world-us-canada-55640427>, last accessed
25 May 2022.

113. For an account of this principle in the context
of financial and other private interests, see e.g.:
Cabinet Office, *Ministerial Code*, pp. 16–19.

114. *The Cabinet Manual*, pp. 2–3.

115. George Jones, *Prime Minister and Cabinet* (Devon:
Wroxton College, 1990).

116. See the discussion at: 'The failure of "good chaps":
are norms and conventions still working in the
UK constitution?', *Institute for Government*
(10 March 2022), available at: <https://
www.instituteforgovernment.org.uk/events/
constitution>, last accessed 2 August 2022.

117. Norman, 'Letter to the Prime Minister'.

118. Dean, 'The Electoral Commission is now under
government control. We should fear for UK
democracy'.

119. Vernon Bogdanor, *Brexit and Our Unprotected
Constitution* (London: Constitution Society, 2018),
available at: <https://consoc.org.uk/wp-content/
uploads/2018/02/Brexit-and-our-unprotected-
constitution-web.pdf>, last accessed 31 July 2022.

120. Cabinet Office, *Findings of the Second Permanent
Secretary's Investigation into Alleged Gatherings on
Government Premises During Covid Restrictions*.

121. Andrew Blick, *The Codes of the Constitution*
(Oxford: Hart, 2016), Chapters 1 and 2.

122. Amy Baker, *Prime Ministers and the Rule Book: The History of Questions of Procedure for Ministers* (London: Politico's, 1999).

123. The Cabinet Office *Precedent Books* are stored and digitised by the National Archive, CAB 181, available at: <https://discovery.nationalarchives.gov.uk/details/r/C15553>, last accessed 25 May 2022.

124. Blick, *The Codes of the Constitution*, pp. 21–2.

125. Hennessy, *The Prime Minister: The Office and its Holders Since 1945*, p. 452.

126. Hazel Armstrong and Chris Rhodes, *The Ministerial Code and the Independent Adviser on Ministerial Interests* (London: House of Commons Library, 2021), p. 38, available at <https://researchbriefings.files.parliament.uk/documents/SN03750/SN03750.pdf>, last accessed 25 May 2022.

127. Lucinda Maer, *The Civil Service Code* (London: House of Commons Library, 2015), p. 7, available at <https://researchbriefings.files.parliament.uk/documents/SN06699/SN06699.pdf>, last accessed 25 May 2022.

128. Pat Strickland, *Committee on Standards in Public Life* (London: House of Commons Library, 2018), pp. 4–5, available at: <https://researchbriefings.files.parliament.uk/documents/SN04888/SN04888.pdf>, last accessed 25 May 2022.

129. An exception is the *Civil Service Code* and related documents which since 2010 have had a statutory basis in the *Constitutional Reform and Governance Act 2010*, Part 1, Section 4.

130. See: Blick, *The Codes of the Constitution*, pp. 242–3.

131. See: Ibid., p. 243.

132. For this view see e.g.: Foreword by the prime minister, Boris Johnson, to the 2019 *Ministerial Code*.

133. Strickland, *Committee on Standards in Public Life*, p. 4.

134. Hennessy, *The Prime Minister: The Office and its Holders Since 1945*, pp. 467–8.

135. Oonagh Gay, *Individual Ministerial Accountability* (London: House of Commons Library, 2012), p. 5, available at: <https://researchbriefings.files. parliament.uk/documents/SN06467/SN06467. pdf>, last accessed 25 May 2022.

136. See e.g.: Peter Walker, 'Ministerial Code: what is it and will it lead to Johnson and Sunak resigning?', *Guardian* (13 April 2022), available at: <https:// www.theguardian.com/politics/2022/apr/13/ ministerial-code-what-is-it-boris-johnson-rishi-sunak-resigning>, last accessed 25 May 2022.

137. Barry K. Winetrobe, *The Accountability Debate: Ministerial Responsibility* (London: House of Commons Library, 1997), pp.16–19, available at: <https://researchbriefings.files.parliament.uk/

documents/RP97-6/RP97-6.pdf>, last accessed
25 May 2022.

138. For an overview see: Blick, *The Codes of the Constitution*, Part 2.

139. Committee on Standards in Public Life, *Upholding Standards in Public Life*, p. 52.

140. Nicholas Reed Langen, 'Should the Ministerial Code have the force of law?', *Prospect* (23 December 2021), available at: <https://www.prospectmagazine.co.uk/politics/should-the-ministerial-code-have-the-force-of-law-boris-johnson-government>, last accessed 25 May 2022.

141. Committee on Standards in Public Life, *Upholding Standards in Public Life*, p. 65.

142. E.g.: Blick, *The Constitution in Review 2*, p. 5.

143. Through, for instance, the Freedom of Information Act 2000.

144. For the *Ministerial Code* and bullying, see: Armstrong and Rhodes, *The Ministerial Code and the Independent Adviser on Ministerial Interests*, p. 46.

145. *Review into the Development and Use of Supply Chain Finance (and Associated Schemes) in Government Part 2: Recommendations and Suggestions* (5 August 2021), p. 4, available at: <https://assets.publishing.service.gov.uk/government/uploads/system/uploads/>

attachment_data/file/1018176/A_report_by_Nigel_
Boardman_into_the_Development_and_Use_
of_Supply_Chain_Finance__and_associated_
schemes__related_to_Greensill_Capital_in_
Government_-_Recommendations_and_
Suggestions.pdf>, last accessed 30 July 2022.

146. House of Commons Select Committee on the
Constitution, 'Corrected oral evidence: The role of
the Lord Chancellor and the law officers' (6 July
2022), p. 36, available at: <https://committees.
parliament.uk/oralevidence/10559/pdf/>, last
accessed 31 July 2022.

147. Meg Russell, 'Brexit and Parliament: The Anatomy
of a Perfect Storm', *Parliamentary Affairs*, 74/2
(April 2021), pp. 443–63, https://doi.org/10.1093/
pa/gsaa011.

148. Daniel Wincott, 'The possible break-up of the
United Kingdom', *UK In A Changing Europe* (19
December 2020), available at: <https://ukandeu.
ac.uk/long-read/the-possible-break-up-of-the-
united-kingdom/>, last accessed 25 May 2022.

149. For a view from the day after the referendum, see:
Laurence Peter, 'Brexit: Five challenges for the
UK when leaving the EU', *BBC News* (24 June
2016), available at: <https://www.bbc.co.uk/news/
uk-politics-eu-referendum-36575186>, last accessed
25 May 2022.

150. Russell, 'Brexit and Parliament'.

151. For analysis of the first Miller case from a variety of perspectives, see: Mark Elliott, Jack Williams, and Alison L. Young (eds), *The UK Constitution After Miller: Brexit and Beyond* (Oxford: Hart, 2018).

152. The prorogation judgment can be found at: <https://www.supremecourt.uk/cases/docs/uksc-2019-0192-judgment.pdf>, last accessed 25 May 2022.

153. Jane Merrick, 'The Queen has been dragged into a constitutional crisis by Boris Johnson over decision to prorogue Parliament', *I* (24 September 2019), available at: <https://inews.co.uk/news/politics/the-queen-latest-constitutional-crisis-boris-johnson-prorogue-parliament-342821>, last accessed 25 May 2022.

154. Armstrong and Rhodes, *The Ministerial Code and the Independent Adviser on Ministerial Interests*, pp. 9–10.

155. Stephen Clear, 'Theresa May was right to reimpose collective responsibility – it's the only way to govern', *The Conversation* (9 July 2018), available at: <https://theconversation.com/theresa-may-was-right-to-reimpose-collective-ministerial-responsibility-its-the-only-way-to-govern-99608>, last accessed 25 May 2022.

156. Gavin Barwell, *Chief of Staff: Notes from Downing Street* (London: Atlantic Books, 2021), p. 171.

157. Stephen Castle, 'As Prime Minister, Boris Johnson Faces the Brexit He Championed', *The New York Times* (23 July 2019), available at: <https://www.nytimes.com/2019/07/23/world/europe/boris-johnson-uk-prime-minister.html>, last accessed 25 May 2022.

158. The most prominent and final defenders of Johnson tended to be notable Brexiteers, most obviously his Cabinet minister Jacob Rees-Mogg. Jon Stone, 'Jacob Rees-Mogg says Boris Johnson should stay PM as he is "a big man who is willing to apologise"', *Independent* (6 July 2022), available at: <https://www.independent.co.uk/news/uk/politics/jacob-reesmogg-boris-johnson-resign-b2116487.html>, last accessed 17 July 2022.

159. Steerpike, 'Is partygate a Remainer plot?', *Spectator* (13 January 2022), available at: <https://www.spectator.co.uk/article/is-partygate-a-remainer-plot->, last accessed 17 July 2022.

160. Andrew Blick and Brian Salter, 'Divided culture and constitutional tensions: Brexit and the collision of direct and representative democracy', *Parliamentary Affairs*, 74/3 (2021), pp. 617–38.

161. See e.g.: Larry Diamond and Marc F. Plattner (eds), *The Global Resurgence of Democracy* (Baltimore: Johns Hopkins University Press, 1996). First edition 1993.

162. Samuel P. Huntington, 'Democracy's third wave', *Journal of Democracy* (1991), 2/2, pp. 12–34; and *The Third Wave: Democratization in the Late Twentieth Century* (Norman: University of Oklahoma Press, 1993).

163. See e.g.: The Economist Intelligence Unit, *Democracy Index 2020* (London: Economist Intelligence Unit, 2020), pp. 3–4.

164. See e.g.: Freedom House, *Democracy in Retreat: Freedom in the World 2019* (Washington: Freedom House, 2019), p. 2

165. For an overview of this concept, see: Stephen Haggard and Robert Kaufman, *Backsliding: Democratic Regress in the Contemporary World* (Cambridge: Cambridge University Press, 2021), Chapter 1.

166. For an overview of the quality of democracy in the United Kingdom, see: Patrick Dunleavy, Alice Park, and Ros Taylor (eds), *The UK's Changing Democracy: The 2018 Democratic Audit* (London: LSE Press, 2018), available at: <https://press.lse.ac.uk/site/books/10.31389/book1/read/?loc=00_Cover.xhtml>, last accessed 26 May 2022.

167. Anne Applebaum, *Twilight of Democracy: The Failure of Politics and the Parting of Friends* (London: Penguin, 2021), pp. 19–20.

168. Committee on Standards in Public Life, *Intimidation in Public Life* (London: Committee

on Standards in Public Life, 2018), available
at: <https://assets.publishing.service.gov.
uk/government/uploads/system/uploads/
attachment_data/file/666927/6.3637_CO_
v6_061217_Web3.1__2_.pdf>, last accessed
26 May 2022.

169. See: Andrew Blick, *Electrified Democracy: The
Internet and the United Kingdom Parliament in
History* (Cambridge: Cambridge University Press,
2021), Chapter 2.

170. Barwell, *Chief of Staff: Notes from Downing
Street*, p. 223.

171. For definitions of populism, see e.g.: Jan
Werner-Müller, *What Is Populism?* (London:
Penguin, 2017); Cas Mudde and Cristóbal Rovira
Kaltwasser, *Populism: A Very Short Introduction*
(Oxford: Oxford University Press, 2017).

172. The former Conservative Party Chairman, Lord
(Chris) Patten, referred in a June 2022 interview
to 'the Johnson cult still hanging on'. See: Tim
Adams, 'Chris Patten: "We have a populist
government that is – fatally – not popular"',
Observer (12 June 2022), available at: <https://
www.theguardian.com/media/2022/jun/12/
chris-patten-we-have-a-populist-government-that-
is-fatally-not-popular>, last accessed 23 June 2022.

173. For criticism of the Civil Service by the most
senior Johnson special adviser, Dominic

Cummings, see: Peter Cardwell, *The Secret Life of Special Advisers* (London: Biteback, 2020), p. 50; see also: Beckie Smith, 'Attorney General's "remain bias" jibe "damaging to civil service morale"', *Civil Service World* (4 July 2022), available at: <https://www.civilserviceworld.com/professions/article/unsubstantiated-criticism-damaging-civil-service-morale-after-attorney-general-slams-remain-bias>, last accessed 29 July 2022.

174. Tom Batchelor, 'Priti Patel's asylum plan will break international law, says UNHCR', *Independent* (23 September 2021), available at: <https://www.independent.co.uk/news/uk/politics/asylum-migrant-bill-priti-patel-unhcr-b1925141.html>, last accessed 30 August 2022.

175. For a flavour of the approach, see e.g.: Ella Glover, 'Boris Johnson "planning reforms which would let ministers overrule judicial decisions"', *Independent* (6 December 2021), available at <https://www.independent.co.uk/news/uk/politics/boris-johnson-reforms-judicial-review-b1970290.html>, last accessed 26 May 2022.

176. See e.g.: Rob Merrick, 'Boris Johnson attacks Parliament for failing "to do anything constructive" as MPs debate domestic violence crackdown', *Independent* (2 October 2019), available at: <https://www.independent.co.uk/news/uk/politics/boris-johnson-conservative-

conference-speech-parliament-attack-domestic-
violence-a9129626.html>, last accessed
26 May 2022.

177. Joint Committee on Human Rights, *Human
Rights Act Reform*, Thirteenth Report of Session
2021–2, HC1033/HL Paper 191 (London: House
of Commons and House of Lords, 2022), p. 4,
available at: <https://committees.parliament.uk/
publications/9597/documents/162420/default/>,
last accessed 26 May 2022.

178. Mason and Allegretti, 'Boris Johnson defies calls to
quit after he and Rishi Sunak fined'.

179. See e.g.: House of Lords Select Committee on the
Constitution, *United Kingdom Internal Market Bill*
(London: House of Lords, London), 17th Report
of Session 2019–21, HL Paper 151, pp. 29–37,
available at: <https://publications.parliament.
uk/pa/ld5801/ldselect/ldconst/151/151.pdf>, last
accessed 26 May 2022; 'UNHCR: UK asylum bill
would break international law, damaging refugees
and global co-operation', *UNHCR*.

180. See e.g.: 'Fourth senior civil servant announces
exit in six months', *BBC News* (9 July 2020),
available at: <https://www.bbc.co.uk/news/
uk-politics-53351672>, last accessed 5 May 2022.

181. Blick, *The Constitution in Review 1*, p. 40.

182. Blick, *The Constitution in Review 2*, pp. 21–2.

183. See e.g.: Haroon Siddique, 'Use of "VIP lane" to

award Covid PPE contracts unlawful, high court rules', *Guardian* (12 January 2022), available at: <https://www.theguardian.com/politics/2022/jan/12/use-of-vip-lane-to-award-covid-ppe-contracts-unlawful-high-court-rules>, last accessed 26 May 2022.

184. For a case of dissemination of misleading information, see e.g.: Sir David Norgrove, chair, UK Statistics Authority, to the prime minister, 'Employment Statistics' (24 February 2022), available at: <https://uksa.statisticsauthority.gov.uk/correspondence/sir-david-norgrove-to-prime-minister-employment-statistics/>, last accessed 26 May 2022.

185. Eduardo Reyes, 'Damning verdict on Raab's Bill of Rights', *The Law Society Gazette* (23 June 2022), available at: <https://www.lawgazette.co.uk/commentary-and-opinion/damning-verdict-on-raabs-bill-of-rights/5112897.article>, last accessed 17 July 2022.

186. Julian Borger, 'UK minister says Northern Ireland protocol threatens Good Friday agreement', *Guardian* (1 June 2022), available at: <https://www.theguardian.com/politics/2022/jun/01/uk-minister-says-northern-ireland-protocol-threatens-good-friday-agreement>, last accessed 17 July 2022.

187. A point central to e.g.: The Rt. Hon. Sir John

Major, 'In Democracy We Trust?', Institute for
Government (10 February 2022), available at:
<https://www.instituteforgovernment.org.uk/
sites/default/files/john-major-in-democracy-we-
trust-100222.pdf>, last accessed 19 May 2022.

188. Morgan Jones, 'Boris Johnson's readiness to
mention deep state conspiracy theories will
have a dangerous ripple effect', *I* (20 July 2022),
available at: <https://inews.co.uk/opinion/
boris-johnson-deep-state-conspiracy-theories-
ripple-effect-1752148>, last accessed 30 July 2022.

189. Lord Frost, 'Observations on the present state
of the nation' (12 October 2021), available at:
<https://www.gov.uk/government/speeches/
lord-frost-speech-observations-on-the-present-
state-of-the-nation-12-october-2021>, last accessed
19 May 2022.

190. Andrew Blick, 'Should we be worried about
democracy in the United Kingdom?', *The
Constitution Society* (11 March 2022), available at:
<https://consoc.org.uk/should-we-be-worried-
about-democracy-in-the-united-kingdom/>, last
accessed 26 May 2022.

191. For a typical view of the UK as stable democracy,
see: Freedom House, 'The United Kingdom',
available at: <https://freedomhouse.org/country/
united-kingdom>, last accessed 26 May 2022.

192. Daniel Ziblatt, *Conservative Parties and the Birth*

of Democracy (Cambridge: Cambridge University Press, 2017), esp. Chapter 1.

193. Examples can be found in e.g.: David Powell, *The Edwardian Crisis: Britain 1901–14* (London: Macmillan, 1996), especially Chapters 2 and 5.

194. For examples of some of the ideas that gestated, see: Douglas Carswell and Daniel Hannan, *The Plan: Twelve Months to Renew Britain* (Douglas Carswell and Daniel Hannan, 2008).

195. Lord Puttnam, 'Power and Fear: the two tyrannies', *Shirley Williams Memorial Lecture* (15 October 2021), available at: <https://www.davidputtnam.com/viewNews/n/lord-puttnam-retirement-full-speech/>, last accessed 19 May 2022.

196. Major, 'In Democracy We Trust?'

197. For an official account of the prime minister, the Cabinet, and their constitutional status, see: Cabinet Office, *The Cabinet Manual*, chapters 3 and 4.

198. For the flexibility of the premiership and the system around it, see: George Jones, *The Power of the Prime Minister: 50 Years On* (London: The Constitution Society, 2016), pp. 11–14, available at: <https://consoc.org.uk/wp-content/uploads/2016/10/The-Power-of-the-Prime-Minister-PDF.pdf>, last accessed 26 May 2020.

199. Blick and Hennessy, *The Hidden Wiring Emerges*, pp. 38–44.

200. Cabinet Office, *Ministerial Code*, p. 3.

201. House of Commons Public Administration Select Committee, *The Prime Minister's Adviser on Ministers' Interests: Independent or Not?*, Twenty Second Report of Session 2010–12, HC 1761 (London: House of Commons, 2012), para. 60, p. 18, available at: <https://publications.parliament.uk/pa/cm201012/cmselect/cmpubadm/1761/1761.pdf>, last accessed 29 July 2022.

202. House of Commons Public Administration Select Committee, *The Prime Minister's Adviser on Ministers' Interests: Independent or Not?*, Oral Evidence (31 January 2012), Sir Alex Allan KCB, independent adviser to the prime minister on ministers' interests, Ev. 11.

203. Armstrong and Rhodes, *The Ministerial Code and the Independent Adviser on Ministerial Interests*, p. 32.

204. Sir Alex Allan, independent adviser on ministerial interests, 'Findings of the Independent Adviser' (20 November 2020), available at: <https://assets.publishing.service.gov.uk/government/uploads/system/uploads/attachment_data/file/937010/Findings_of_the_Independent_Adviser.pdf>, last accessed 29 July 2022.

205. 'Ministerial Code Investigation', *GOV.UK* (20 November 2020), available at: <https://www.gov.uk/government/news/ministerial-code-investigation>, last accessed 29 July 2022.

206. 'Statement from Sir Alex Allan', *GOV.UK* (20 November 2020), available at: <https://www.gov.uk/government/news/statement-from-sir-alex-allan>, last accessed 30 July 2022.

207. 'Priti Patel quits cabinet over Israel meetings row', *BBC News* (8 November 2017), available at: <https://www.bbc.co.uk/news/uk-politics-41923007>, last accessed 30 July 2022.

208. For a selection, see: Gavin Cordon, 'Boris Johnson: Three decades of scandals, blunders and rows', *Independent* (12 January 2022), available at: <https://www.independent.co.uk/news/uk/boris-johnson-jennifer-arcuri-priti-patel-prime-minister-michael-howard-b1991890.html>, last accessed 26 May 2022; Jamie Grierson, 'Lies, damned lies: the full list of accusations against Boris Johnson', *Guardian* (10 December 2021), available at: <https://www.theguardian.com/politics/2021/dec/10/lies-accusations-boris-johnson-full-list-dishonesty-christmas-party>, last accessed 26 May 2022.

209. Josh Halliday, 'Scandal after scandal: timeline of Tory sleaze under Boris Johnson', *Guardian* (1 July 2022), available at: <https://www.theguardian.

com/politics/2022/jul/01/scandal-timeline-tory-sleaze-boris-johnson>, last accessed 17 July 2022.

210. Kuenssberg, 'Boris Johnson: The inside story of the prime minister's downfall'.

211. For a discussion of Johnson as clown, see: Edward Docx, 'The clown king: how Boris Johnson made it by playing the fool', *Guardian* (18 March 2021), available at: <https://www.theguardian.com/news/2021/mar/18/all-hail-the-clown-king-how-boris-johnson-made-it-by-playing-the-fool>, last accessed 26 May 2022.

212. Terry Eagleton, 'Boris Johnson is no clown', *UnHerd* (30 March 2022), available at: <https://unherd.com/2022/03/boris-johnson-is-no-clown/>, last accessed 26 May 2022.

213. Nigel Warburton, 'Why shaming Boris Johnson for his self-serving antics is unlikely to work', *The New European* (18 November 2021), available at: <https://www.theneweuropean.co.uk/why-boris-johnson-is-like-diogenes-of-sinope/>, last accessed 26 May 2022.

214. Michael Gove, 'Portrait', in Boris Johnson, *The Essential Boris Johnson: Lend Me Your Ears* (London: Harper Perennial, 2004), pp. 2–3.

215. Boris Johnson, *Have I Got Views For You* (London: Harper Perennial, 2008), pp. 431–2.

216. See e.g.: George Parker, Sebastian Payne, and Jasmine Cameron-Chileshe, 'Boris Johnson vows

he will not quit as he awaits "partygate" report',
Financial Times (26 January 2022), available at:
<https://www.ft.com/content/1e625e52–224f-46fa-
8bf9–4a12ea2394b1>, last accessed 27 May 2022.

217. Stone, 'Jacob Rees-Mogg says Boris Johnson
should stay PM as he is "a big man who is willing
to apologise"'.

218. Johnson, *Have I Got Views For You,* pp. 431–2.

219. Alan Duncan, *In the Thick of It: The Private Diaries
of a Minister* (London: William Collins, 2021),
diary entry for 24 September 2017, p. 227.

220. Sonia Purnell, 'Boris Johnson wants us to see
him as a modern day Churchill. Don't fall for
it', *Prospect* (10 November 2017), available at:
<https://www.prospectmagazine.co.uk/politics/
boris-johnson-wants-us-to-see-him-as-a-modern-
day-churchill-dont-fall-for-it>, last accessed
27 May 2022.

221. Boris Johnson, *The Churchill Factor: How One
Man Made History* (London: Hodder &
Stoughton, 2014), p. 124.

222. Jessica Elgot, 'Scottish Tory leader withdraws
letter of no confidence in Boris Johnson',
Guardian (10 March 2022), available at: <https://
www.theguardian.com/politics/2022/mar/10/
scottish-tory-leader-withdraws-letter-of-no-
confidence-in-boris-johnson>, last accessed
27 May 2022.

223. Toby Helm, Phillip Inman, and James Tapper, '"We got the big calls right" said Boris Johnson. But did he really?', *Guardian* (30 January 2022), available at: <https://www.theguardian.com/ politics/2022/jan/30/we-got-the-big-calls-right-said-boris-johnson-but-did-he-really>, last accessed 17 July 2022.

224. Allegretti, 'Supreme Court judges could be vetted by MPs in wake of prorogation ruling'; Jones, 'Boris Johnson's readiness to mention deep state conspiracy theories will have a dangerous ripple effect'.

225. Johnson, *The Essential Boris Johnson: Lend Me Your Ears*, p. 300.

226. Rajeev Syal, 'Priti Patel's Rwanda asylum seeker plan faces first legal challenge', *Guardian* (27 April 2022), available at: <https://www.theguardian. com/politics/2022/apr/27/priti-patel-faces-legal-challenge-over-rwanda-asylum-seeker-plan>, last accessed 27 May 2022.

227. Boris Johnson, *Seventy-Two Virgins* (Harper, London, 2004), p. 231.

228. Ibid., p.215.

229. 'The Guardian view on the Gray report: a diagnosis of sick government', *Guardian* (25 May 2022), available at: <https://www. theguardian.com/commentisfree/2022/may/25/

the-guardian-view-on-the-gray-report-a-diagnosis-of-sick-government>, last accessed 27 May 2022.
230. Harry Mount (ed.), *The Wit and Wisdom of Boris Johnson* (London: Bloomsbury Continuum, 2019), p. 79.
231. Ibid., p. 83.
232. See e.g.: Laura Kuenssberg, 'Partygate: Insiders tell of packed No10 lockdown parties', *BBC News* (24 May 2022), available at: <https://www.bbc.co.uk/news/uk-politics-61566410>, last accessed 25 May 2022.
233. Blick, *The Constitution in Review 2*, pp. 12–17.
234. For an example of a robust defence, see the secretary of state for digital, culture, media, and sport Nadine Dorries in a Channel 4 news interview broadcast on 31 January 2022, available at: <https://www.channel4.com/news/the-prime-minister-tells-the-truth-says-nadine-dorries>, last accessed 15 June 2022.
235. For an account that shows such an awareness, see: Cardwell, *The Secret Life of Special Advisers* (London: Biteback, 2020), p. 108.
236. Andrew Mitchell, *Beyond a Fringe: Tales From a Reformed Establishment Lackey*, loc. 3106.
237. Albert Evans, 'Michael Howard is "not sure" if he was right to sack Boris Johnson for lying when he was Tory leader', *I* (11 July 2019), available at: <https://inews.co.uk/news/politics/

michael-howard-boris-johnson-sacked-tory-leadership-election-latest-news-312600>, last accessed 31 July 2022.

238. 'Gove's leadership bid statement in full', *Guardian* (30 June 2016), available at: <https://www.theguardian.com/politics/2016/jun/30/goves-leadership-bid-statement-in-full>, last accessed 17 July 2022.

239. Duncan, *In the Thick of It*, diary entry for 24 September 2017, p. 227.

240. Jane Martinson, 'Why did the Daily Mail support Johnson long after other press allies turned their backs?', *Guardian* (7 July 2022), available at: <https://www.theguardian.com/commentisfree/2022/jul/07/boris-johnson-daily-mail-press-allies>, last accessed 17 July 2022.

241. For analysis of Johnson's career from this perspective, see: Tom McTague, 'Why Boris Johnson gets away with it', *The Atlantic* (16 April 2022), available at: <https://www.theatlantic.com/international/archive/2022/04/boris-johnson-ukraine-covid-lockdown-party/629576/>, last accessed 27 May 2022.

242. Michael Savage, 'Fears grow over Boris Johnson win as Hunt challenge fades', *Observer* (6 July 2019), available at: <https://www.theguardian.com/politics/2019/jul/06/

boris-johnson-win-fears-hunt-challenge-fades-tories-conservatives>, last accessed 17 July 2022.

243. For a recent popular account of such networks, see: Simon Kuper, *Chums: How a Tiny Caste of Oxford Tories Took Over the UK* (London: Profile, 2022).

244. Kate Fall, *The Gatekeeper* (London: HQ, 2020), p. 174.

245. Sasha Swire, *Diary of an MP's Wife: Inside and Outside Power* (London: Abacus, 2021), loc. 6689.

246. Ibid., loc. 6693–6701.

247. Duncan, *In the Thick of It*, diary entry for 24 September 2017, p. 227.

248. On the astonishing tenacity of Johnson, see: Martin Kettle, 'This munity should be the end of Johnson. But never underestimate his sheer lust for power', *Guardian* (6 July 2022), available at: <https://www.theguardian.com/commentisfree/2022/jul/06/boris-johnson-resignations-lust-for-power>, last accessed 17 July 2022.

249. Gaby Hinsliff, 'Boris Johnson sacked by Tories over private life', *Guardian* (14 November 2004), available at: <https://www.theguardian.com/politics/2004/nov/14/uk.conservatives>, last accessed 31 July 2022.

250. Lionel Barber, *The Powerful and the Damned: Life Behind the Headlines in Financial Times*

(London: Penguin, 2021), diary entry for 24 July 2019, p. 422.

251. Conservative Party, *Get Brexit Done, Unleash Britain's Potential: The Conservative and Unionist Party Manifesto 2019*, pp. 47–8.

252. Reproduced in Mark Francois, *Spartan Victory: The Inside Story of the Battle for Brexit* (privately published, 2021), Appendix 4.

253. Christian Calgie, 'Steve Baker "seize power"' [video] YouTube (8 July 2022), available at: <https://www.youtube.com/watch?v=xr-ZY3DUUys>, last accessed 25 September 2022.

254. For the ERG decision to back Johnson for the leadership and the reservations members had, see: Francois, *Spartan Victory*, p. 326. See also: Cardwell, *The Secret Life of Special Advisers*, p. 183.

255. They include: Suella Braverman, Priti Patel, and Anne-Marie Trevelyan; *Spartan Victory*, Appendix 1, 3.

256. Dominic Raab, *The Assault on Liberty: What Went Wrong with Rights* (London: Fourth Estate, 2009).

Part Two: The Problem in Detail

1. For a discussion of public discourse and democracy, see: Peggy Ruth Geren, 'Public discourse: Creating the conditions for dialogue

concerning the common good in a postmodern heterogeneous democracy', *Studies in Philosophy and Education*, 20/3 (2001), pp. 191–9.

2. Boris Johnson, *The Dream of Rome* (London: Harper Perennial, 2007), e.g.: 'The Single Currency', pp. 175–9.

3. Johnson, *The Churchill Factor*, p. 28.

4. 'Brexit: Boris Johnson warns against "punishment beatings"', *BBC News* (18 January 2017), available at: <https://www.bbc.co.uk/news/uk-politics-38658998>, last accessed 17 July 2022.

5. 'Boris Johnson compares Ukraine war to Brexit vote', *BBC News* (19 March 2022), available at: <https://www.bbc.co.uk/news/av/uk-politics-60810168>, last accessed 17 July 2022.

6. Conservative Party, *Get Brexit Done, Unleash Britain's Potential: The Conservative and Unionist Party Manifesto 2019*, p. 3.

7. David Blevins, 'The PM said there would be "no checks" but there will be', *Sky News* (20 May 2020), available at: <https://news.sky.com/story/johnsons-deal-for-northern-ireland-is-not-what-was-agreed-11991803>, last accessed 26 August 2022.

8. See e.g.: O'Carroll, 'Dominic Cummings says UK always intended to ditch NI protocol'; O'Carroll, 'Boris Johnson promised to tear up NI protocol, says DUP MP Ian Paisley'.

9.   Andrew Blick, 'Weaponising the Exit Agreement: the ongoing Irish dimension of Brexit', *Federal Trust* (20 May 2020), available at: <https://fedtrust.co.uk/weaponising-the-exit-agreement-the-ongoing-irish-dimension-of-brexit/>, last accessed 17 July 2022.

10. Campbell, 'Brexit: EU says UK grace period extension breaches international law'.

11. Arj Singh, 'Brexit: UK threatens to trigger Article 16 sparking EU warning as Northern Ireland Brexit talks stall', *I* (5 November 2021), available at: <https://inews.co.uk/news/politics/brexit-latest-uk-threatens-to-trigger-article-16-as-northern-ireland-brexit-talks-stall-sparking-eu-warning-1287187>, last accessed 28 August 2022.

12. House of Lords Select Committee on the Constitution, *United Kingdom Internal Market Bill*, pp. 29–37.

13. Alice Tidey, 'Brexit: EU's "heavy-handed actions" have lost support for Northern Ireland protocol, says Lord Frost', *euronews* (5 October 2021), available at: <https://www.euronews.com/2021/10/04/brexit-eu-s-heavy-handed-actions-have-lost-support-for-northern-ireland-protocol-says-lord>, last accessed 26 August 2022.

14. Borger, 'UK minister says Northern Ireland protocol threatens Good Friday agreement'.

15. For analysis, see: O'Toole, 'Britain's attack on

its own protocol is one more exercise in Brexit gaslighting'.

16. Wright, 'Priti Patel inquiry: Boris Johnson condemned for refusing to throw cabinet bully overboard'.

17. Mason and Allegretti, 'Boris Johnson defies calls to quit after he and Rishi Sunak fined'.

18. 'Chancellor Rishi Sunak held US green card until last year', *BBC News* (8 April 2022), available at: <https://www.bbc.co.uk/news/uk-politics-61044847>, last accessed 14 June 2022.

19. For an insertion on bullying and harassment, see: *Ministerial Code*, para 1.2.

20. Carole Cadwalladr and Emma Graham-Harrison, 'Boris Johnson's key adviser must face sanction, demand MPs', *Guardian* (28 July 2019), available at: <https://www.theguardian.com/uk-news/2019/jul/28/dominic-cummings-must-face-sanctions-demand-leading-mps>, last accessed 14 June 2022.

21. *Memorandum of Understanding between the Cabinet Office and the UK Statistics Authority* (London: Cabinet Office/UK Statistics Authority, April 2020), p. 2, available at: <https://assets.publishing.service.gov.uk/government/uploads/system/uploads/attachment_data/file/882373/MoU_-_Cabinet_Office_UK_Statistics_Authority.pdf>, last accessed 19 June 2022.

22. 'Response from Sir David Norgrove to Alistair

Carmichael MP – Use of official crime statistics by Prime Minister, Home Secretary and Home Office'.

23. *Ministerial Code* (London: Cabinet Office, 2022).

24. Ibid., paras 1.4–1.7.

25. Cabinet Office, *Findings of the Second Permanent Secretary's Investigation into Alleged Gatherings on Government Premises During Covid Restrictions*.

26. 'Statement from Sir Alex Allan'.

27. 'Boris Johnson "forgot" about Chris Pincher groping claims'.

28. Mason and Allegretti, 'Boris Johnson defies calls to quit after he and Rishi Sunak fined'.

29. House of Commons Public Administration and Constitutional Affairs Committee, email from Lord Geidt received on 17 June 2022, available at: <https://committees.parliament.uk/publications/22732/documents/167114/default/>, last accessed 17 July 2022.

30. For general concerns on this point see: ibid. See also e.g.: House of Lords Select Committee on the Constitution, *United Kingdom Internal Market Bill*, pp. 29–37.

31. Joint Committee on Human Rights, *Human Rights Act Reform*, p. 4.

32. Evans, 'The government should go beyond a "low level of ambition" on the Ministerial Code'.

33. Blick, *The Constitution in Review 2*, p. 21.

34. Mason, 'New chancellor Zahawi tells Johnson to go as Donelan quits after 48 hours in job'.

35. Blick, *The Constitution in Review 2*, p. 25.

36. Lizzie Dearden, 'Misleading the country: Boris Johnson and ministers have made dozens of false statements to Parliament', *Independent* (19 April 2022), available at: <https://www.independent.co.uk/news/uk/politics/boris-johnson-false-statements-parliament-b2060800.html>, last accessed 17 July 2022.

37. 'Commons Privileges Committee investigation into Boris Johnson', *Institute for Government* (5 July 2022), available at: <https://www.instituteforgovernment.org.uk/explainers/privileges-committee-investigation>, last accessed 17 July 2022.

38. Conn, 'Matt Hancock acted unlawfully by failing to publish Covid contracts'.

39. Jones, 'The Northern Ireland Protocol Bill: legal (and perhaps illegal) goings on".

40. Independent adviser on ministers' interests, *Annual Report* (May 2021), paras 20–34.

41. Richard Wheeler, 'Gove denies levelling-up funding "abuse" amid concerns raised by MPs', *Independent* (24 January 2022), available at: <https://www.independent.co.uk/news/uk/michael-gove-boris-johnson-mps-prime-minister-

andrew-bridgen-b1999636.html>, last accessed 18
July 2022.

42. Steve Goodrich (ed.), *Track and Trace: Identifying
Corruption Risks in UK Public Procurement for
the Covid-19 Pandemic* (London: Transparency
International, 2021), available at: <https://
www.transparency.org.uk/sites/default/files/
pdf/publications/Track%20and%20Trace%20
-%20Transparency%20International%20UK.
pdf>, last accessed 18 July 2022, pp. 6–7; House
of Commons Committee of Public Accounts,
*Government's Contracts with Randox Laboratories
Ltd*, p. 3.

43. Wheeler, 'Gove denies levelling-up funding
"abuse" amid concerns raised by MPs'.

44. For a discussion, see: Martin Stanley, 'Dismissal:
permanent secretaries', *Understanding the Civil
Service* (2021), available at: <https://www.
civilservant.org.uk/information-dismissal-
permanent_secretaries.html>, last accessed 18
July 2022.

45. Boris Johnson, *Life in the Fast Lane: The Johnson
Guide to Cars* (London: Harper Perennial,
2007), p. 8.

46. Johnson, *Life in the Fast Lane*, pp. 19–21.

47. For an example of incredulous international
coverage of the claim by Conservative MP Conor
Burns that Johnson was 'ambushed with a cake',

see: Jennifer Hassan, 'Was Boris Johnson birthday partying in lockdown or "ambushed with a cake"? Britons mock the latest defence', *The Washington Post* (26 January 2022), available at: <https://www.washingtonpost.com/world/2022/01/26/boris-johnson-lockdown-party-ambushed-by-cake/>, last accessed 18 July 2022.

48. The Supreme Court, R (on the application of Miller) (Appellant) *v* The Prime Minister (Respondent) Cherry and others (Respondents) *v* Advocate General for Scotland (Appellant) (Scotland).

49. All-Party Parliamentary Group on Democracy and the Constitution, *An Independent Judiciary*, pp. 18–19.

50. 'Covid: Government's PPE "VIP lane" unlawful, court rules', *BBC News*.

51. Conn, 'Matt Hancock acted unlawfully by failing to publish Covid contracts'.

52. See e.g.: 'Half of VIP lane companies supplied PPE worth £1billion that was not fit for purpose', *Spotlight on Corruption* (11 February 2022), available at: <https://www.spotlightcorruption.org/half-of-vip-lane-companies-supplied-ppe-worth-1-billion-that-was-not-fit-for-purpose/>, last accessed 18 July 2022.

53. Michael Holden and Kylie Maclellan, 'PM Johnson escapes further fines as London police

end "partygate" inquiry', *Reuters* (19 May 2022), available at: <https://www.reuters.com/world/uk/uk-police-end-downing-street-party-inquiry-126-fines-issued-2022–05–19/>, last accessed 18 July 2022.

54. For a discussion of this issue, see: Clive Coleman, 'Could Tony Blair face legal action over Iraq War?', *BBC News* (7 July 2016), available at: <https://www.bbc.co.uk/news/uk-36738086>, last accessed 2 August 2022.

55. 'Northern Ireland Protocol Bill: UK government legal position', *GOV.UK* (13 June 2022), available at: <https://www.gov.uk/government/publications/northern-ireland-protocol-bill-uk-government-legal-position/northern-ireland-protocol-bill-uk-government-legal-position>, last accessed 2 August 2022.

56. Hansard, House of Commons Debates (8 September 2020), cols 499; 508–9, available at: <https://hansard.parliament.uk/commons/2020-09-08/debates/2F32EBC3-6692-402C-93E6-76B4CF1BC6E3/NorthernIrelandProtocolUKLegalObligations>, last accessed 23 June 2022.

57. Andrew Blick, 'The Conservative constitutional turn', *The Constitution Society Blog* (13 June 2022), available at: <https://consoc.org.uk/

the-conservative-constitutional-turn/>, last
accessed 18 July 2022.

58. Lisa James, 'The Queen's Speech, the Johnson
government, and the constitution – lessons from
the 21–22 session', *The Constitution Society Blog*
(19 May 2022), available at: <https://consoc.org.
uk/the-queens-speech-the-johnson-government-
and-the-constitution-lessons-from-the-2021-22-
session/>, last accessed 18 July 2022.

59. Edward Scott, 'House of Lords appointments:
should the process be reviewed?', *House of Lords
Library* (12 November 2021), available at: <https://
lordslibrary.parliament.uk/house-of-lords-
appointments-should-the-process-be-reviewed/>,
last accessed 18 July 2022.

60. Rajeev Syal, 'Boris Johnson and Prince Charles
to hold Rwanda talks', *Guardian* (22 June 2022),
available at: <https://www.theguardian.com/
uk-news/2022/jun/22/boris-johnson-and-prince-
charles-to-hold-rwanda-talks>, last accessed 18
July 2022.

61. Kaya Burgess, '"Immoral" Rwanda policy shames
Britain, say archbishops', *The Times* (13 June
2022), available at: <https://www.thetimes.co.uk/
article/immoral-rwanda-policy-shames-britain-
say-archbishops-bg55d7gmo>, last accessed 18
July 2022.

62. See e.g.: Peter Walker and Heather Stewart, 'BBC

staffed by people "whose mum and dad worked there", says Nadine Dorries', *Guardian* (4 October 2021), available at: <https://www.theguardian.com/politics/2021/oct/04/bbc-staffed-by-people-whose-mum-and-dad-worked-there-says-nadine-dorries>, last accessed 30 August 2022; Ian Burrell, 'How big a threat does Nadine Dorries pose to the BBC?', *New Statesman* (29 November 2021), available at: <https://www.newstatesman.com/politics/media/2021/11/how-big-a-threat-does-nadine-dorries-pose-to-the-bbc>, last accessed 30 August 2022.

63. Jim Waterson, 'BBC funding "up for discussion", says Nadine Dorries, as licence fee frozen', *Guardian* (17 January 2022), available at: <https://www.theguardian.com/media/2022/jan/17/no-final-decision-made-on-bbc-licence-fee-says-nadine-dorries>, last accessed 18 July 2022.

64. See e.g.: the notorious blog by Dominic Cummings, published while he was serving as the most senior special adviser to Boris Johnson, '"Two hands are a lot" – we're hiring data scientists, project managers, policy experts, assorted weirdos…' (2 January 2020), available at: <https://dominiccummings.com/2020/01/02/two-hands-are-a-lot-were-hiring-data-scientists-project-managers-policy-experts-assorted-weirdos/>, last accessed 29 July 2022.

65. See e.g.: Ibid; Smith, 'Attorney General's "remain bias" jibe "damaging to civil service morale"'.

66. Jim Dunton, 'Home Office's settlement with ex-perm sec topped £370k', *Civil Service World* (9 July 2021), available at: <https://www.civilserviceworld.com/news/article/home-office-settlement-with-philip-rutnam-priti-patel-topped-370k>, last accessed 29 July 2022.

67. *Civil Service Code* (London: Civil Service, 2015), available at: <https://www.gov.uk/government/publications/civil-service-code/the-civil-service-code>, last accessed 19 June 2022.

68. Cabinet Office, *Findings of the Second Permanent Secretary's Investigation into Alleged Gatherings on Government Premises During Covid Restrictions*, p. 8.

69. 'Partygate: Which Downing Street parties have resulted in fines?', *BBC News* (27 May 2022), available at: <https://www.bbc.co.uk/news/uk-politics-60124162>, last accessed 18 July 2022.

70. The Rt Hon Lord Geidt, independent adviser on ministers' interests to the prime minister, 'Refurbishment works at 11 Downing Street' (17 December 2021), available at: <https://assets.publishing.service.gov.uk/government/uploads/system/uploads/attachment_data/file/1044951/lord-geidt-to-prime-minister-17-december-2021.pdf>, last accessed 18 July 2022.

71. House of Commons Committee of Public Accounts, *Government's Contracts with Randox Laboratories Ltd*, p. 3.

72. Cohen, 'Former civil servant bulldozes through No 10's defence of disgraced MP Chris Pincher'.

73. See e.g.: Andrew Woodcock, 'Dominic Cummings leaks WhatsApp exchange suggesting Boris Johnson called Matt Hancock "totally f****** hopeless"', *Independent* (16 June 2021), available at: <https://www.independent.co.uk/news/uk/politics/cummings-boris-hancock-whatsapp-b1866973.html>, last accessed 18 July 2022.

74. Peter Walker, '"Truth twisters": rogue civil service tweet causes storm', *Guardian* (24 May 2020), available at: <https://www.theguardian.com/politics/2020/may/24/can-you-imagine-having-to-work-with-these-truth-twisters>, last accessed 18 July 2022.

75. Cabinet Office, *Findings of the Second Permanent Secretary's Investigation into Alleged Gatherings on Government Premises During Covid Restrictions*, p. 11.

76. Parsley and Merrick, 'Home Office civil servants challenged "callous" Rwanda migrant policy'.

77. Cabinet Office, *Findings of the Second Permanent Secretary's Investigation into Alleged Gatherings*

on Government Premises During Covid Restrictions, p. 36.

78. 'PM statement on the Sue Gray report: 31 January 2022', *GOV.UK*, available at: <https://www.gov.uk/government/speeches/pm-statement-on-the-sue-gray-report-31-january-2022>, last accessed 1 August 2022.

79. Ibid.

80. 'Declaration on Government Reform' (15 June 2021), available at: <https://assets.publishing.service.gov.uk/government/uploads/system/uploads/attachment_data/file/993902/FINAL_Declaration_on_Government_Reform.pdf>, last accessed 1 August 2021.

81. Blick, *The Constitution in Review 1*, p. 30.

Part Three: Recommendations and Conclusion

1. Lord Evans, 'The government should go beyond a "low level of ambition" on the Ministerial Code': *Ministerial Code*, para. 1.4, pp. 2–3; 'Statement of government policy: standards in public life', *GOV.UK* (27 May 2022), available at: <https://www.gov.uk/government/publications/revisions-to-the-ministerial-code-and-the-role-of-the-independent-adviser-on-ministers-interests/>

statement-of-government-policy-standards-in-public-life>, last accessed 2 August 2022.

2. See the discussion at: 'The failure of "good chaps": are norms and conventions still working in the UK constitution?'.

3. *Review into the Development and Use of Supply Chain Finance (and Associated Schemes) in Government Part 2: Recommendations and Suggestions.*

4. All-Party Parliamentary Group on Democracy and the Constitution, *An Independent Judiciary: Challenges Since 2016*, pp. 56–9.

5. They are: the Committee on Standards in Public Life; the Electoral Commission; the Independent Parliamentary Standards Authority; the Boundary Commission for England; and the Parliamentary Commissioner for Standards. Robert Hazell, Marcial Boo, and Zachariah Pullar, *Parliament's Watchdogs: Independence and Accountability of Five Constitutional Regulators* (London: The Constitution Unit, 2022), p. 6, available at: <https://www.ucl.ac.uk/constitution-unit/sites/constitution_unit/files/195_parliaments_watchdogs_july_2022_0.pdf>, last accessed 30 July 2022.

6. Committee on Standards in Public Life, *Upholding Standards in Public Life*. For a summary of proposals, see pp. 13–17.

7. Committee on Standards in Public Life, *Upholding Standards in Public Life*, pp. 52–3.

8. Blick, *The Codes of the Constitution*.

9. [2021] EWHC 3279 (Admin), Case No: CO/618/2021 (6 December 2021), para. 39, available at: <https://www.judiciary.uk/wp-content/uploads/2021/12/FDA-v-Prime-Minister-judgment-061221.pdf>, last accessed 30 July 2022.

10. Blick, *The Constitution in Review 2*, pp. 13–14.

11. House of Lords Select Committee on the Constitution, 'Corrected oral evidence: Role of the Lord Chancellor and the law officers' (23 March 2022), p. 42, available at: <https://committees.parliament.uk/oralevidence/9937/pdf/>, last accessed 30 July 2022.

12. House of Commons Select Committee on the Constitution, 'Corrected oral evidence: Role of the Lord Chancellor and the law officers' (6 July 2022), p. 36, available at <https://committees.parliament.uk/oralevidence/10559/pdf/>, last accessed 28 September 2022.

13. See e.g.: Blick, *The Constitution in Review 1*, pp. 49–52.

14. See e.g.: Brice Dickson, *Writing the United Kingdom Constitution* (Manchester: Manchester University Press, 2019).

15. See e.g.: Nicholas W. Barber, 'Against a written constitution', *Public Law* 2/1 (2008).

16. Bogdanor, *Brexit and Our Unprotected Constitution*.

17. House of Lords Select Committee on the Constitution, 'Corrected oral evidence: Role of the Lord Chancellor and the law officers' (22 June 2022), pp. 30–1, available at: <https://committees. parliament.uk/oralevidence/10467/pdf/>, last accessed 30 July 2022.

Appendices

1. Committee on Standards in Public Life, *Upholding Standards in Public Life: Final Report of the Standards Matter 2 Review* (London: Committee on Standards in Public Life, 2021), pp. 13–17.

2. For a small selection of relatively recent titles, see: Mark Bennister, 'The contemporary UK prime minister. When the personal becomes political: Agency, character, personality and celebrity', *Asian Journal of Comparative Politics* (2022), available at: <https://journals.sagepub.com/ doi/10.1177/20578911221106351>, last accessed 26 September 2022; Andrew Blick and George Jones, *Premiership: The Development, Nature and Power of the British Prime Minister* (Exeter: Imprint

Academic, 2010); Christopher Byrne and Kevin Theakston, 'Understanding the power of the prime minister: Structure and agency in models of prime ministerial power', *British Politics*, 14/4 (2019), pp. 329–46; Patrick Diamond, *Governing Britain: Power, Politics and the Prime Minister* (London: Bloomsbury, 2013); Keith Dowding, 'The prime ministerialisation of the British prime minister', *Parliamentary Affairs*, 66/3 (2013), pp. 617–35; Richard Heffernan, 'Exploring (and explaining) the British prime minister', *The British Journal of Politics and International Relations*, 7/4 (2005), 605–20; Hennessy, *The Prime Minister: The Office and its Holders Since 1945*; Sue Pryce, *Presidentializing the Premiership: The Prime Ministerial Advisory System and the Constitution* (London: Palgrave Macmillan, 1997).

3. For a classic text in this area, see: R. A. W. Rhodes and Patrick Dunleavy (eds), *Prime Minister, Cabinet and Core Executive* (London: Macmillan, 1995). See also: Robert Elgie, 'Core executive studies two decades on', *Public Administration*, 89/1 (2011), pp. 64–77; Richard Heffernan, 'Prime ministerial predominance? Core executive politics in the UK', *The British Journal of Politics and International Relations*, 5/3 (2003), pp. 347–72.

4. Important entries in this field include: Vernon

Bogdanor, *The New British Constitution* (Oxford: Hart, 2009); Anthony King, *The British Constitution* (Oxford: Oxford University Press, 2007); Jonathan Sumption, *Trials of the State: Law and the Decline of Politics* (London: Profile, 2019).

5. E.g.: Maria Sobolewska and Robert Ford, *Brexitland: Identity, Diversity and the Reshaping of British Politics* (Cambridge: Cambridge University Press, 2020); Alison Young, 'The Constitutional Implications of Brexit', *European Public Law*, 23/4 (2017).

6. E.g.: Natasha Lindstaedt, *Democratic Decay and Authoritarian Resurgence* (Bristol: Bristol University Press, 2021).

7. Applebaum, *Twilight of Democracy*; Pippa Norris and Ronald Inglehart, *Cultural Backlash: Trump, Brexit, and Authoritarian Populism* (Cambridge: Cambridge University Press, 2019); Alison Young, 'Populism and the UK Constitution', *Current Legal Problems*, 71/1 (2018), pp. 17–52.

8. For analysis of such texts in context, see: Blick, *The Codes of the Constitution*; and Blick and Hennessy, *The Hidden Wiring Emerges*.